MYTHS, MEMORIES, AND THE REPRESENTATION OF IDENTITIES

Acclaim for other Peter Burke titles previously published by EER.

Secret History and Historical Consciousness.
From The Renaissance To Romanticism.

"Burke characteristically mixes seemingly opposing approaches – historical truth and fiction, oral and print sources, elite and folk tastes, mega- and micro history, symbolic and literal readings, private and public knowledge – to reveal their coexistence and interaction. He revisits received views with neglected or newly discovered sources and aperçus, not to overturn but to enlighten and amplify. Burke makes arcane topics of daunting complexity relevant and readily accessible in remarkable feats of translation from past to present. Familiarity with an extraordinary range of multilingual sources is couched in graceful and self-effacing prose, consistently instructive and entertaining."
– **David Lowenthal**, *Times Literary Supplement*, 7 April 2017.

"*Secret History* is a timely collection in which Peter's Burke's many strengths as a cultural historian are all on display: intellectual independence, restless curiosity, a willingness to seek out questions others have ignored, and a mastery of the early modern period and its legacy. It's also beautifully written. Anyone interested in intellectual history or the making of modern Europe will find this a deeply rewarding read."
– **James Shapiro**, Professor of English, Columbia University, author of *1606: Shakespeare and the Year of Lear*.

"His erudition is enviable, and his lucid, effortless presentation exemplary."
– **John Pemble**, joint winner of the Wolfson Prize for *The Mediterranean Passion*.

Also available by Peter Burke from *EER*:

History as Spectacle. Charles V and imagery

What is History Really About? Reflections on Theory and Practice

Secret History and Historical Consciousness. From the Renaissance to Romanticism

Identity, Culture and Communications in the Early Modern World

MYTHS, MEMORIES, AND THE REPRESENTATION OF IDENTITIES

Peter Burke
*Emeritus Professor of Cultural History,
Emmanuel College, Cambridge.*

EER
Edward Everett Root, Publishers, Brighton, 2019.

EER

Edward Everett Root, Publishers, Co. Ltd.,
30 New Road, Brighton, Sussex, BN1 1BN, England.
www.eerpublishing.com

edwardeverettroot@yahoo.co.uk

Details of our overseas Agencies are given on our website.

Peter Burke, *Myths, Memories, and The Representation of Identities*

First published in Great Britain in 2019.
© Peter Burke 2019.
This edition © Edward Everett Root 2019.

ISBN hardback   978-1-912224-83-8
ISBN paperback 978-1-912224-82-1
ISBN eBook   978-1-912224-84-5

Peter Burke has asserted his right to be identified as the author of this Work in accordance with the Copyright, Designs and Patents Act 1988 as the owner of this Work.

All rights reserved. No part of this publication may be reproduced, stored in a retrieval system or transmitted in any form or by any means, electronic, mechanical, photocopying, recording or otherwise, without the prior permission of the copyright owner.

Cover design by Pageset Limited. Book production by Head & Heart.
Printed in Great Britain by TJI Limited, Padstow, Cornwall.

Contents

Acknowledgements..vii
Introduction...ix

Part 1, Myths
 1. The Myth of the Iron Crown...1
 2. The Myth of the Borgias..9
 3. Foundation Myths and Collective Identities in Early Modern
    Europe...19
 4. Myths of Venice...31
 5. History, Myth and Fiction: Doubts and Debates................47

Part 2, Memories
 6. Co-memorations: performing the past...............................77

Part 3, Representations
 7. The Director as Historian: Rossellini's Louis XIV.............97
 8. The Reconstruction of Political Rituals in the Age of
    Louis XIV..109
 9. On the Margins of the Public and the Private: Louis XIV at
    Versailles..125
 10. Representing Women's Work in Early Modern Italy.........137

ACKNOWLEDGEMENTS

The author and publishers gratefully acknowledge the permission of those publications in which the original chapters previously appeared in books or in journals, as follows: Part 1, Myths. The Myth of the Iron Crown, published in Italian in *La Corona Ferrea* 1, ed. G. Buccellati (Milan, Mondadori, 1995), 3-8. This is the original English version; The Myth of the Borgias (previously unpublished); 'Foundation Myths and Collective Identities in Early Modern Europe', in *Europe and the Other and Europe as the Other*, ed. Bo Stråth (Brussels, Peter Lang, 2000), 113-22; 'Myths of Venice', in Katia Pizzi and Godela Weiss-Sussex (eds.) *The Cultural Identities of European Cities* (Oxford: Peter Lang, 2010), 77-92; 'History, Myth and Fiction: Doubts and Debates', *Oxford History of Historical Writing* vol.3, ed. J. Rabasa, M. Sato, E. Tortarolo, D. Woolf (Oxford, Oxford University Press, 2012), 261-81. Part 2, Memories. 'Co-memorations: performing the past', in Karin Tilmans, Frank van Vree and Jay Winter (eds.) *Performing the Past: memory, history and identity in modern Europe* (Amsterdam: Amsterdam University Press, 2010, 105-18. Part 3, Representations. 'The Director as Historian: Rossellini's Louis XIV', previously unpublished. 'The Reconstruction of Political Rituals in the Age of Louis XIV', French translation in *Le Protocole ou La mise en forme de l'ordre politique*, ed. Yves Deloye, Claudine Haroche et Olivier Ihl (Paris-Quebec, L'Harmattan, 1996), 171-83. Here we print the original English version. 'On the Margins of the Public and the Private: Louis XIV at Versailles', *International Political Anthropology* 2 (2009), 29-36; Representing Women's Work in Early Modern Italy', in Josef Ehmer and Catharina Lis (eds.) *The Idea of Work in Europe from Antiquity to Modern Times* (Farnham, Ashgate, 2009), 177-87.

Introduction

This fourth volume of my essays brings together both published and previously unpublished papers on three related topics: myths, memories and representations.

As the introductions to several of these essays explain, I reject the binary opposition between history and myth, equated with truth and falsehood.[1] I prefer to use the term 'myth' in the sense of a story in which the protagonists are larger than life, whether they are heroes or villains, golden or dark ages. The cases that most interest me are concerned with events that actually happened in the past, which are mythologized in varying degrees when they are recalled and narrated. The events are made more dramatic and so more memorable, while complex events are 'condensed', as Freud wrote of dreams, becoming simpler ones.

A famous example of this process of mythologization is the story that the Renaissance (viewed as an event rather than a process) happened because when the Ottoman sultan Mehmet II captured Constantinople in 1453, Greek scholars fled to Italy and taught their Italian colleagues to read ancient Greek and to love Plato and Homer. Some Greek scholars did indeed flee at this time and teach their language and philosophy in Italy, France and elsewhere, but others had arrived in Western Europe

---

[1] Hence some historians employ the hybrid term 'mythistory': William H. McNeill, 'Mythistory', *American Historical Review* 91 (1986), 1-10; Joseph Mali, *Mythistory* (Chicago, 2003).

Myths, Memories, and The Representation of Identities

long before, while Italian humanists had already made study trips to Constantinople and returned laden with manuscripts.[2]

Another example of condensation is the attribution of discoveries made by second-rank scholars and scientists to more famous ones, a practice described by the sociologist Robert Merton as 'the Matthew Effect' (since the Gospel according to Matthew declares that 'to him who hath will be given').[3] More exactly, a discovery is remembered as the work of Galileo, Newton or Einstein because their names are more familiar. In a word, the memory is mythologized, and Galileo and others become heroes of the quest for knowledge.

It has long been noted by folklorists and others that some myths are based on older ones and that different saints, for instance, share the same basic biography. More recently, some oral historians decided to carry out a second round of interviews decades after the first one, asking the same witnesses about the same events and comparing the two versions of the stories that they provided. On the second occasion, the stories were increasingly mythologized, closer to stories that these individuals once read or heard or saw on screen.[4]

The mythologization of events is clear in partisan histories or in organized commemorations, reminding us of a famous definition of myth as a story about the past that justifies or legitimates a state of affairs in the present. For example, the story of Guy Fawkes, discussed in chapter 6, was used to justify discrimination against Catholics in Britain and Ireland. Alternatively, a myth may 'delegitimate' or demonize a particular social group, as in stories of plots by Jews or Jesuits.[5]

---

[2] Peter Burke, 'The Myth of 1453: Notes and Reflections', *Querdenken: Dissens und Toleranz im Wandel der Geschichte: Festschrift Hans Guggisberg*, ed. Michael Erbe et al. (Mannheim 1996), 23-30.
[3] Robert Merton, 'The Matthew Effect in Science', *Science* 159 (1968), 56-63.
[4] Alessandro Portelli, *The Death of Luigi Trastulli and other stories: form and meaning in oral history* (Albany NY, 1991); Alastair Thomson, *Anzac Memories: Living with the Legend* (Melbourne, 1994).
[5] 'The Black Legend of the Jesuits: an Essay in the History of Social Stereotypes', *Christianity and Community in the West: Essays for John Bossy*, ed. Simon Ditchfield (Aldershot, 2001), 165-82, reprinted in my EER volume *Secret History and Historical Consciousness*, ch.12.

Introduction

Both myths and memories are forms of 'representation', a useful general term that includes texts, images and rituals and has been employed more and more frequently since the journal *Representations* was founded in 1983. Several essays in this collection deal with the public images of rulers, Louis XIV and the emperor Charles V.[6] These representations are analysed in terms of the famous five questions formulated by the American polymath Harold Lasswell, 'Who says What, Which channel, to Whom, with What effects?', adding two additional questions suggested by one of Lasswell's critics, 'For What purpose?' and 'Under What circumstances?'[7]

The final essay turns to images of working women in early modern Italy, using these representations as a source to supplement the scarcity of evidence for this work in official documents. As in the case of texts, images need to be submitted to the process of source criticism by historians, a process something like cross-examination in court – except that the images cannot answer back. All the same, they provide information about the past that it is impossible to recover by other means.[8]

---

[6] Another essay, not reprinted here, is 'Images de trois rois: François Ier entre Charles Quint et Henri VIII', in , B. Petey-Girard and M. Vène (eds.) *François Ier: pouvoir et image* (Paris, 2015, 25-43.
[7] Lyman Bryson (ed.) *The Communication of Ideas* (New York, 1948), 37-51; Richard Braddock, 'An Extension of the Lasswell Formula', *Journal of Communication* 8 (1958), 88-93.
[8] Peter Burke, *Eyewitnessing* (London, 2001) discusses this form of evidence in more detail.

1: THE MYTH OF THE IRON CROWN

This chapter is concerned not so much with the history of the iron crown itself but with its place in what historians call 'the collective imaginary' or 'social memory'. In other words, the topic to be discussed here is what might be called the 'myth' of the crown.[1]

Historians, especially positivist historians, often use the term 'myth' in a purely negative sense, to mean a story which – according to them – is not true. Here, however, I would prefer to follow the lead of students of literature and anthropology and use the term in a more positive sense, as a story – whether true or not – with a symbolic meaning.

Myths are often told to explain why the world is as it is, and especially to justify or 'legitimate' particular political or social arrangements. In stories of this kind the protagonists are larger than life, whether they are heroes or villains, and wonders occur, frequently associated with material objects such as rings, caps or swords (Arthur's Excalibur, Roland's Durendal, Charlemagne's Joyeuse, and so on).

Myths often follow a stereotyped form. The same story floats or wanders from one protagonist and one location to others,

---

[1] The German historian Reinhard Elze wrote about the 'Legende', 'Sage', or 'Fabel' of the crown. Since this essay was first published in 1995, a general history of the crown has appeared: Valeriana Maspero, *La corona ferrea. La storia del più antico e celebre simbolo del potere in Europa* (Monza, 2003).

or fragments into independent stories which may in turn be combined with others. In other words, a myth is a magnet attracting other myths.

In these stories, characters or events often come in threes (the Danish folklorist Axel Olrik called this the 'rule of three'). One naturally thinks of the three kings, or magi, who brought presents to the infant Christ, and according to one tradition, are buried in Milan.[2] Or of the three rings – symbolizing Judaism, Christianity and Islam – which a father gave to his three sons in the famous story in Boccaccio's *Decameron*, which a sixteenth-century Italian miller Menocchio Scandella, retold to his interrogators following his arrest by the Inquisition.[3]

It will be obvious that the story of the iron crown of Lombardy, kept in the cathedral of Monza, a small town in Milan, is a myth according to the definition or description offered above. The famous crown is one of three, made in three different metals – iron, silver and gold – and associated with three cities, Aachen, Monza (or Milan) and Rome, and three bishops – the archbishop of Mainz, the archbishop of Milan, and the pope.[4] It is associated with heroes and heroines who are larger than life, among others with Julius Caesar, St Helena, Queen Theodelinda, and Charlemagne.

The crown is also associated with the relic of the holy nail, and with other wonders. When, for example, the crown, with other objects from the treasury of Monza, had been taken to Avignon, so the story goes, an attempt to steal the treasure was foiled by a miracle (stories of this kind about treasures and relics were common in the Middle Ages). The thief 'saw armed men who according to him mounted guard on the treasure' [*vide visibilmente huomini armati, quali a lui parvero facessero la guardia à esso Thesoro*][5] Finally, the story of the crown is a means of glorifying the city of

---

[2] Paolo Morigia, *Historia dell'antichità di Milano* (Venice, 1592), 339.
[3] Giovanni Boccaccio, *Decameron*, Book One, the third story; Carlo Ginzburg, *The Cheese and the Worms* (1976: English translation, Baltimore 1992), 23.
[4] Carlo Sigonio, *Historiarum de regno Italiae libri xv* (Venice, 1574), 288. There is also a version of the story with only two crowns, for example in Ptolemy of Lucca (iron at Milan, gold at Rome) or a brief of Pope Innocent VII in 1355 (iron at Milan, silver at Aachen).
[5] Gianfrancesco Besozzo, *Historia Pontificale di Milano* (Milan, 1623), 200.

Monza, of reminding people that it was once as important as its successful rival Milan.

So far I have retold the story of the crown as if it were timeless, in the way in which myths are told in oral tradition. It is time to try to insert it in history. My aim in this short essay is not to present the history of the crown – this has been provided by scholars who are much better qualified than I am to do so. My aim is simply to present the history of the myth of the crown. In fact this task is not as simple as it may appear to be. Myths do indeed change over time. They have to do so in order to continue to legitimate political and social arrangements which are themselves subject to change.

On the other hand, oral traditions leave few traces. All we have are a few written versions of stories which were probably current in thousands of oral forms. It is possible to arrange the written versions in chronological order and to examine the ways in which they have changed, as I intend to do, but the reader must bear in mind the fact that these written versions are an extremely small sample of the total. New elements of the story may only appear in writing generations after they began to circulate by word of mouth.

The myth of the crown appears to be a composite of at least three stories which might be entitled the 'Crown of Monza', the 'Iron crown', and the 'Holy Crown'. Let us look at them in order.

Like Milan, Pavia and Verona, Monza was one of the cities closely associated with the Lombard rulers of the sixth, seventh and eighth centuries. It was associated in particular with Queen Theodelinda, a Bavarian princess who married King Agilulfo in 590. The Lombards were Arian in religion but Theudelinda was Catholic. We know from the history of the Lombards written by Paul the Deacon in the eighth century that Theudelinda built a church in Monza (now the cathedral) and gave it treasure.[6] Her tomb is still to be seen there.

After a gap of about three centuries, we hear of three emperors being crowned at Monza: Corrado II in 1093, Corrado III in 1128, and Federico I Barbarossa in 1155. By the thirteenth century, if not

---

[6] Paul the Deacon, *History of the Lombards* (English translation, Philadelphia PA, 1974), Book 4, ch.21.

before, the story of the three imperial crowns, the three metals and the three cities was in circulation, told by Jacopo da Varazze, best known as the author of the *Golden Legend*, a famous collection of stories, or myths, of the saints. There are later references to gold and silver crowns associated with Monza, a silver crown used to crown Charlemagne, for instance, and golden crowns worn by Agilulfo and Theodelinda. It is obvious enough that the story of the crown of Monza contributed to the glory of the city, 'the head of Lombardy and the seat of the kingdom' [*caput Lombardiae et sedes regni*], as the emperor Frederick 'Barbarossa' described Monza in 1159; 'the most noble land of Monza' [*la nobilissima Terra di Monza*] according to the Milanese cleric Paolo Morigia, and 'imperial city' according to the local author Bartolomeo Zucchi (who also described Queen Theodelinda, the iron crown and San Gherardo as the 'three most illustrious glories of Monza').

The crown of Monza was not always described as iron, and the iron crown, to which we now turn, was not always associated with Monza. According to Tolomeo of Lucca, for example, it was to be found in Milan. There are several thirteenth-century references to an iron crown at Monza, one of them in an inventory of the treasures of the cathedral. Yet in 1311, the emperor Henry VII is said to have searched for the crown in both cities without success, while others say he was crowned with the iron crown at Milan. In 1355, the emperor Charles IV was also crowned with an iron crown – at Monza according to the chroniclers Giovanni and Matteo Villani, but at Milan according to the poet Petrarch.

By the fourteenth century, if not before, the iron crown was associated with the Roman emperors and the choice of iron rather than a more noble metal was explained as a symbol of conquest. As Villani put it, 'Just as iron and steel tame every other metal, so the emperors ... will tame ...all the nations of the world' [*Come l'acciaro et ferro doma ogni altro metallo, cosi i Cesari ... domaro ... tutte le nationi del mondo*].[7] The chronicler Bernardino Corio gave the same explanation. 'Julius Caesar, Octavian and Trajan were the first to be crowned with the iron crown because they

---

[7] Quoted in Rocco Bombelli, *Storia della Corona Ferrea* (1870), 218.

had subjugated the world with iron' [*Della corona di ferro furon coronati prima Cesare, Ottaviano, & Traiano perche havevano col ferro soggiogato l'universo*].[8] The crown was also associated with Charlemagne, who drove the Lombards from Italy. The appeal of the crown to Charles V, who was crowned with it at Bologna in 1530, and to Napoleon, who crowned himself with it at Milan in 1805, was surely that these men saw themselves and were seen by others as second Charlemagnes.

Matteo Villani wrote of `The Holy Crown of Iron'. The third element in the myth of the crown was that it was, or contained, a holy relic. Already in the fourth century St Ambrose, bishop of Milan, told the story of Santa Elena, mother of the emperor Constantine, finding not only the true cross but the nails used to crucify Christ, and making a diadem of one of them, which Constantine wore. Villani's words suggest that the iron crown was already identified with that diadem.

However, the cult of the iron crown of Monza as one of the holy nails is attested from the later sixteenth century onwards. The Portuguese Jesuit Emanuele Sa, preaching in Milan in the presence of the archbishop, San Carlo Borromeo, quoted Ambrose and claimed that the Monza crown 'was the very one that Constantine wore' [*fosse quella propria portò Constantino*].[9] When San Carlo Borromeo carried out his visitation of Monza, he ordered the relics associated with Theodelinda to be placed in a more honourable setting.[10] The inventory of the treasure of Monza made in 1590 refers to the 'iron circlet which is said to have been made from one of Our Lord's nails' [*circulus ferreus quem aiunt constructum ex uno clavorum Domini*].[11] The seventeenth-century historian Bartolomeo Zucchi adds the detail that it was Pope Gregory who gave Queen Theodelinda 'The IRON crown of Constantine the Great (which contains one of the holy nails' [*la corona FERREA, quella che fù del Magno Costantino (che in se rinchiude*

---

[8] Bernardino Corio, *L'historia di Milano* (Venice, 1565), 64.
[9] Besozzo, Historia, 106.
[10] Bartolomo Zucchi, *Tre illustrissime glorie di Monza* (Milan, 1613), 37.
[11] Magda von Bárány-Oberschall, *Die eiserne Krone der Lombardei* (Vienna, 1966), 45.

uno de'sagri chiodi].¹² Another historian, Gianfrancesco Besozzo, was more detached, quoting the story told by St Ambrose but 'leaving the verdict to the pious reader'.

In 1684, Cardinal Litta placed the crown in a special chapel for public veneration, and in 1717 a papal committee, the *Sacra Congregazione de' Riti*, confirmed the cult, including the carrying of the relic in procession every September to be exposed for three days on the high altar of the cathedral of Monza. Nevertheless, like Besozzo and the inventory of 1590, the *Congregazione* did not commit itself to the authenticity of the nail, described as 'piously believed to be one of the nails of our Lord Jesus Christ' [*una ex Clavis Domini Nostri Jesu Christi, ut piè creditur*]. In 1797, however, in the protest at its seizure, the circlet was described as 'one of the principal relics of our religion'.

Why the cult of the holy nail, transformed into a circlet, should have developed in the later sixteenth century is an interesting question. Earlier in the century, Calvin's famous attack on relics had maliciously listed fourteen holy nails to be found in Rome, Paris and elsewhere, but Monza was not mentioned. In the later sixteenth century, however, Carlo Borromeo encouraged the cult of the holy nail of Milan, said to have been discovered by St Ambrose and presented to the city by the emperor Theodosius. In 1576, when Milan was struck by plague, San Carlo, 'inspired by God, took this most holy nail from its place and inserted it in a great wooden cross' [*spirato da Dio, levò questo santissimo Chiodo dal suo luoco, & lo ripose in una gran Croce di legno*], which was taken in procession. As a result, 'The plague came to an end'.¹³ Should one interpret the cult of the nail at Monza as an expression of the city's rivalry with Milan? Or would it be more accurate to see it as an example of the spiritual empire of San Carlo?

It is worth lingering for a moment, in conclusion, on Queen Theodelinda. As we have seen, her friendship with pope Gregory the Great and her foundation of a church at Monza were chronicled by Paul the Deacon. In the fourteenth century,

---

¹² Zucchi, *Tre glorie*, 20, with a marginal reference to an unnamed 'grave auttore'.
¹³ Morigia, *Historia*, 339.

the best-known reference to 'Teudelinga' comes from Boccaccio's *Decameron*, where she is portrayed as `a most beautiful and wise and extremely honourable lady, but unlucky in love'.[14] In the fifteenth century, on the other hand, Theodelinda was glorified in a series of frescoes by the brothers Zavattini showing that the story of the queen being guided by St John the Baptist in a dream to the place where the church should be built was already in oral circulation.[15]

In the later sixteenth century, as the cult of the holy nail grew in importance, Theodelinda was virtually turned into a saint. For the historians Gasparo Bugati and Paolo Morigia she was 'holy' [*santa*].[16] For Bartolomeo Zucchi, who wrote her biography, Theodelinda was 'a most Catholic queen'.[17] Although she was not canonized, the anniversary of her death on 22 January was celebrated in Monza.[18]

If we regard myths as stories about the past which are told in order to legitimate political and social arrangements in the present, it is not difficult to explain the rise of the image of the saintly queen at the time of the Counter-Reformation. According to Corio and Morigia the queen restored much property that the Church had lost, while bishops were honoured in her time. For his part, Zucchi claimed that she had converted her husband Agilulfo and the Lombards to Catholicism.[19] At a time when heretics again threatened the faith and princes were taking property from the Church, the story of Theodelinda was relevant to the present as never before.

---

[14] Boccaccio, Book One, the second story.
[15] The story is told in G. Bugati, *Historia universale* (Venezia, 1571), 145.
[16] *Bugati*, Historia, 149; Morigia, *Historia*, 27.
[17] Zucchi, *Tre glorie*, 7.
[18] Zucchi, *Tre glorie*, 46.
[19] Corio, *Historia*, 25; Morigia, *Historia*, 27; Zucchi, *Tre glorie*, 18.

2: THE MYTH OF THE BORGIAS AND THE MYTH OF THE RENASISSANCE

Historians, especially, perhaps, in the empiricist culture of the Anglophone world, tend to use the word 'myth' to refer to a story about the past which is not true, contrasting it with the real 'history' they write themselves. Some recent and typical book titles in English include 'the myth of Soviet military supremacy'; '1940: myth and reality'; and 'Paul Macartney, the man behind the myth'.[1]

Michel Foucault accused historians of having what he called an 'impoverished' or 'thin' idea of the real, which excluded the imagined and other realities. In similar but more precise fashion, the definition of myth which I have just offered might also be criticized as too 'thin' as well as too negative, since it defines myth exclusively in terms of what it is not. Literary critics, social anthropologists and psychologists, among others, work with much richer, more positive and more complex conceptions of myth, which are of great relevance to the study of the past. There have been many discussions of this topic, and many controversies, far too many to summarize here.[2]

---
[1] T. Gervasi, *The Myth of Soviet Military Supremacy* (New York, 1986); Clive Ponting, *1940: Myth and Reality* (London, 1990); R. Benson, *Paul Macartney: the Man behind the Myth* (London, 1992).
[2] Percy Cohen, 'Theories of Myth', *Man* (1969), 337-53.

All that can reasonably be done at this point is to make a few general remarks that are particularly relevant to historians of the Renaissance in particular. Hence I shall make no distinction between myths and legends but simply draw attention to three essential characteristics of a certain kind of story about the past.

1. A myth is a story of marvellous or extra-ordinary events in which the protagonists are larger than life, with superhuman qualities, whether they are heroes or villains. Indeed the protagonists represent, embody or symbolize values, making them concrete and so more memorable.

2. A myth is a story composed of schemata, recurrent elements which wander or float from one story or one protagonist to another.

3. A myth is a story about the past with the function of legitimating or de-legitimating something in the present – (hence a 'sacred' story, with a taboo against questioning it).

It should be noted that 'falsehood' or even 'inaccuracy' is not part of the definition. What a historian who traces the development over time of a given story will often notice, however, is what might be called a process of 'mythification'. As a given story is told again and again, whether by word of mouth or in writing, it diverges more and more from the sources, and in the process it gradually acquires the characteristics of a myth. The divergence is not random but affected by the desires and fears (conscious or unconscious) of the people who pass the story on.

I shall argue that the story of the Renaissance is a myth in the sense of the term defined above. To be more precise, there have been a number of myths of the Renaissance, beginning in the period itself (with Machiavelli, Guicciardini, Vasari, and so on), and continuing to the present time. I am not, of course, asserting that the socio-cultural movement we call the Renaissance did not take place. Still less do I imply that Leonardo da Vinci or Cesare Borgia did not exist. What I do wish to argue is that the story of the Renaissance, as it has been told and retold from the fifteenth century to our own day, contains the three essential characteristics or criteria which have just been mentioned.

We may begin with the Renaissance myth of the Renaissance. The story of the `Renaissance', a term already used on occasion in the sixteenth century, is a story in which the protagonists are larger than life, like Leonardo or the 'divine' Michelangelo. The movement was often presented as a kind of miracle, a creation *ex nihilo* with the aid of divine Providence. It was also viewed as a movement from darkness to light, for it was the Renaissance humanists who invented the idea of the 'Dark Ages'.[3]

The story of the Renaissance is also a story composed of prefabricated elements or schemata. At the macro-level, for instance, the story of the 'rebirth' of learning and the arts is a secular version of the story of Christianity, including the need to be born again 'by water and the Holy Ghost'. At the micro-level, we might turn to the lives of the artists as told by Giorgio Vasari and others. It has been pointed out more than once that these lives resemble the lives of the saints as told in the *Golden Legend* for example, in the sense that different artists share the same biography, or more exactly that particular anecdotes, stories or 'mythemes' (as Lévi-Strauss called them) wander from one artist to another.[4] Take for example the story of the discovery of the artistic talent of a peasant boy, who is found drawing with a stick in the sand, or with a stone on a rock, or with a piece of coal on a wall. This story is told with only minor variations in the biographies of Giotto, Castagno, and Beccafumi in Giorgio Vasari's *Lives* (1550).

In the third place, the story of the Renaissance sometimes has the function of legitimation. In the case of Vasari, whose lives of artists was published by the official printer of the Grand Duke Cosimo de' Medici, in whose service Vasari made his career, the myth of a golden age associated with the Medici before 1494 is clear enough.

---
[3] Lucie Varga, *Das Schlagwort vom finsterer Mittelalter* (Vienna, 1932).
[4] Ernst Kris and Otto Kurz, *Legend, Myth and Magic in the Image of the Artist* (1934: English translation, New Haven 1979); Paul Barolsky, *Michelangelo's Nose: a Myth and its Maker* (Philadelphia PA, 1990).

Other sixteenth-century stories of the Renaissance have the opposite function, de-legitimation, notably the stories about Italy and Italians current in Protestant Europe, in which 'Popery' was associated with immorality, Machiavelli with atheism, and so on. The theatre of Shakespeare's England furnishes some literally dramatic examples, from Christopher Marlowe's *Jew of Malta*, in which Machiavelli comes on stage to open the play, to 'revenge' tragedies such as John Webster's *The White Devil* and *The Duchess of Malfi*. Revenge, like poison, was seen – by northern Europeans at least – as especially Italian, as in the case of the 51st story in the *Heptameron* of Marguerite de Navarre.

If we turn to the nineteenth century, whether it is to imaginative writers like Alfred de Musset (*Lorenzaccio*, 1834), Victor Hugo (*Lucrèce Borgia*, 1833), or George Eliot (*Romola*, 1863), or to historians such as Jules Michelet (*La Renaissance*, 1855), Jacob Burckhardt (*Die Cultur der Renaissance*, 1860), or Ferdinand Gregorovius (*Lucrezia Borgia*, 1874), we find new elements in the myth of the Renaissance, notably the emphasis on cultural traits such as realism, individualism, many-sidedness, as well as on ruthlessness and violence. The English critic Walter Pater summed up the change when he described himself as giving the term 'a much wider scope than was intended by those who originally used it to denote that revival of classical antiquity in the fifteenth century which was only one of many results of a general excitement and enlightening of the human mind'.[5] However, in this case too the collective story of the movement, or period, can be said to satisfy our three criteria.[6]

In the first place, the protagonists of the drama of the Renaissance were still viewed as larger than life, whether as heroes or villains or a combination of the two. Alfred de Musset painted a vivid portrait of Lorenzino de'Medici, George Eliot did the same for Savonarola, and so on. Robert Browning condensed his age's view of the Renaissance into brilliantly vivid images in a number of dramatic poems of the 1840s about individuals

[5] Walter Pater, *The Renaissance* (London, 1873), xii.
[6] Wallace K. Ferguson, *The Renaissance in Historical Thought* (Cambridge MA, 1948); J. B. Bullen, *The Myth of the Renaissance in 19th-Century Historical Writing* (Oxford, 1994).

who are also social types, notably the worldly cleric ('The bishop orders his tomb in St Praxed's'), and the ruthless but art- loving ruler ('My last Duchess').

In the second place, the stories contained recurrent elements. Heroes and villains were presented not only as individuals but as the embodiment of certain values attributed to the Renaissance, notably 'realism' (in a broad range of meanings), worldliness, the aesthetic attitude to life (as opposed to a moral one) and finally individualism. Paradoxically, nineteenth-century images of Renaissance men and women look alike precisely because of the stress on their individualism (not only in the sense of 'uniqueness' of course, but also freedom from social restraints, self-consciousness and the drive to emulate others).

As for the legitimating function of the myth of the Renaissance, it is less obvious and also less precise than in the case of the sixteenth century. The main point is that the Renaissance was (and still is) presented as an essential part of the 'grand narrative' of the rise of modernity in the west. As Burckhardt famously put it, the Renaissance Italian was 'the first-born among the sons of modern Europe'. In this way the story of the Renaissance miracle helped and helps to justify western claims to superiority, to 'civilization'. It also helped and helps to legitimate modernity, at least a certain kind of modernity, a function it has been performing since the great battle between the ancients and the moderns at the end of the seventeenth century.[7]

For example, consider the Renaissance image of the Borgias. On the positive side, we might regard the work of the painter Pinturicchio and the scholar-forger Giovanni Nanni as contributions to the creation of a Borgia myth. Nanni linked the Borgias to a certain 'Romus', the 20th king of Spain, who founded Valencia. Romus also went to Italy and enlarged the settlement which was later to be known as 'Rome'. As for Pinturicchio, or his humanist adviser (if he had one), in his frescoes in the Appartamento Borgia in the Vatican he combined the bull of the

---

[7] Jacob Burckhardt, *The Civilization of the Renaissance in Italy* (1860: English translation, new edition, Harmondsworth 1990); Hans Blumenberg, *The Legitimacy of the Modern Age* (1966: English translation, Cambridge MA 1983).

Borgia family coat of arms with Apis, the bull worshipped by the ancient Egyptians.[8]

Again, the apparently cool, detached analyst Machiavelli made an important contribution to the myth of Cesare Borgia in the famous seventh chapter of his *Prince*, where Cesare was presented as a major exemplar of political skill or *virtù*. As the Italian scholar Gennaro Sasso demonstrated a number of years ago, a comparison between Machiavelli's first impressions of Cesare when he met him in 1502 with his later account in the *Prince* shows an individual turning into a symbol, an exemplum, the illustration of a general thesis.[9] In similar fashion Machiavelli's account of the trick played on Vitellozzo Vitelli and others at Sinigaglia was mythologized in the sense that the final version, the *Modo tenuto*, presented Cesare as completely in control of the situation, in a way that Machiavelli's original reports had not done.

As for the negative image of the Borgias, it had a good deal to do with Julius II's dislike of his papal predecessor, and it received a classic and influential exposition in the *Storia d'Italia* of Francesco Guicciardini. At the beginning of his history, Guicciardini painted a vivid portrait of pope Alexander VI that was modelled on Livy's portrait of Hannibal, itself a good example of historical myth-making.[10] Guicciardini – like Paolo Giovio in his *History of his Own Time* – also helped to associate the name 'Borgia' with poison in his famous account of the death of the pope. 'According to the most common rumour' [*secondo la fama più comune*] wrote Guicciardini with his customary caution, Alexander accidentally drank wine from a flask which Cesare had had poisoned in order to kill the cardinal of Corneto.[11]

Other historians were less prudent. For example, the professional writer Francesco Sansovino, in his *Chronology of the World*, first published in 1580, included the laconic entry 'Alexander VI died of poison'. The Protestant writer John Foxe

---
[8] Fritz Saxl, 'The Appartamento Borgia', in his *Lectures* (London, 1957), 174-88.
[9] Gennaro Sasso, *Machiavelli e Cesare Borgia* (Rome, 1966).
[10] Francesco Guicciardini, *Storia d'Italia*, Book 6, chapter 4 (1561-4: ed. Constantino Panigada, Bari 1929).
[11] Guicciardini, *Storia*, Book 5, chapter 6.

claimed that Alexander was poisoned at his dinner table when a servant brought him the wrong bottle by mistake. The pope's death by poison was dramatized by another Englishman, Barnabe Barnes, in *The Divils Charter* (1607).[12]

In what follows I shall concentrate on the theme of poison, because in England and France at least, this was and remains the best-remembered part of the myth. In France, for example, in a poem published in 1558, Joachim Du Bellay associated Italians with poison.[13] In England, in 1592, the writer Thomas Greene also associated Italians with 'strange poisonings'.[14] In the tragedies of John Webster, early in the seventeenth century, 'Italians poison their victims in four distinct ways: by the leaves of a book, the lips of a picture, the pommel of a saddle and an anointed helmet'.[15] To what extent English and French readers derived their idea of Italians as poisoners from Guicciardini's account of the Borgias is difficult to say, but his *History of Italy* was quite well-known in those countries (translations into French and English were published in the sixteenth century). But the crucial point is that the Borgias (like Machiavelli) came to represent Italy for those Europeans (especially Protestant northerners) who hated and feared Italian culture.

Voltaire was sceptical of the idea that Alexander VI had been poisoned as he was sceptical of much received history.[16] In the nineteenth century, however, Ranke, Michelet and Burckhardt all accepted the story. In his history of the popes, Ranke asserted quite simply that Alexander 'died of the poison he had destined for another'.[17] As for Burckhardt, he emphasized what he called the 'devilish wickedness' of Cesare (viewing it as an extreme example of a general trend of the period). The fascination which this unscrupulous man of action held for the Swiss scholar can be seen in Burckhardt's speculation about what might have

---

[12] Joscelyn N. Hillgarth, 'The Image of Alexander VI and Cesare Borgia in the Sixteenth and Seventeenth Centuries', *Journal of the Warburg and Courtauld Institutes* 59 (1996), 119-29.
[13] Joachim Du Bellay, *Les Regrets* (Paris, 1558), no. 127.
[14] Thomas Greene, *A Quip for an Upstart Courtier* (London, 1592), folio Ci, recto.
[15] John R. Hale, *England and the Italian Renaissance* (1954: second edn. London 1963), 23.
[16] Voltaire, *Essai sur les Moeurs* (Paris, 1751), chs. 110-111.
[17] Leopold von Ranke, *History of the Popes* (1834-6: English translation, 4th edn, London 1866), Book 1, ch.2; Jules Michelet, *La Renaissance* (Paris, 1855), chs 6-7.

happened in the next conclave had Cesare not been ill at the very moment when his father died. 'In pursuing such a hypothesis the imagination loses itself in an abyss'.[18] Burckhardt was brought up as a Swiss Protestant, and some traces of the tradition of Protestant suspicion of Italy can be detected in his work.

However, the difference between the sixteenth- and the nineteenth-century myths of the Borgias are more important than the similarities. In the sixteenth-century, the Borgias had represented a part of Europe, Italy, and more especially (at least for Protestants), Rome. In the nineteenth century, however the family came to represent a period, the Renaissance. Stendhal had made the point even more explicitly than Burckhardt when he called Cesare 'the representative of his century', a demonic century of passion and genius.[19]

Of course, some nineteenth- and twentieth-century historians have shared Voltaire's scepticism and indeed went beyond him in the critique of Guicciardini and others. The historian of the popes, Ludwig von Pastor, noted that accounts of Alexander's death reveal the symptoms of malaria, and criticized Ranke for his 'strange pertinacity' in adhering to the 'untenable theory' of poison.[20]

My favourite example of skepticism is an English one, the writer Lacy Collison-Morley, whose idea it was to test the hypothesis that the Borgias were great poisoners by compiling statistics of the deaths of cardinals under four consecutive popes. He concluded that twenty-seven cardinals died in the thirteen-year reign of Sixtus IV; eight, in the eleven-year reign of Innocent VIII; twenty-seven, in the eleven-year reign of Alexander VI; and thirty-six, in the nine-year reign of Julius II.[21] So one cardinal a year, more or less, died under Innocent, two a year under Sixtus, two and a half a year under Alexander, and four a year under Julius.

---

[18] Burckhardt, *Civilization*, 90.
[19] Stendhal, *Histoire de la peinture en Italie* (Paris, 1817), quoted in Ferguson, *Renaissance*, 130.
[20] Ludwig von Pastor, *History of the Popes*, vol. 6 (English translation, London 1898), 135.
[21] Lacy Collison-Morley, *The Story of the Borgias* (London, 1932), 234-8. Cf J. H. Whitfield, 'New Views upon the Borgias', *History* 29 (1944), 77-88.

The Myth of the Borgias and the Myth of the Renasissance

Even this elegant demonstration was not enough to prevent the old story from continuing to circulate. When I was a child, the humorous weekly *Punch* used to carry regular historical cartoons by the artist George Morrow. I still remember one representing a couple in Renaissance costume planning a dinner, and the wife saying to her husband: 'I don't think I'll invite the Borgias. They might feel they have to ask us back'.[22] In this trivialization of the myth, the name 'Borgia' has become little more than a symbol for 'poisoner'. All the same, the cartoon teaches us an important lesson. It reminds us of one of the best-known features of myth, which is that once a story of this kind has been launched, it is virtually impossible to eliminate it, even after the reasons for the fabrication of the original story have long disappeared. The Borgia myth is supported by, as in turn it supports, a popularized romantic vision of a violent and passionate Renaissance.

---

[22] https://punch.photoshelter.com/gallery/George-Morrow.../G0000OWV778h5Fd8

3: Foundation Myths and Collective Identities in Early Modern Europe

The aim of this chapter is to discuss the use of the past in the formation of collective identities, taking its illustrations from Europe in the early modern period, from the Renaissance to the Enlightenment, in other words looking at collective identities before the age of nationalism. In this period there existed a large family of stories about the origins of social groups and institutions, stories which like a range of material objects from (the regalia of monarchs, ancestral tombs, the Roman ruins surviving in certain cities, and so on) served to support collective identities, although they are now regarded by historians – in Eric Hobsbawm's famous phrase – as invented traditions.[1]

The importance, in the early modern period as in the Middle Ages, of 'legitimation by descent', is clearly shown by these stories or myths. 'Myth' is of course a slippery, ambiguous term. In the following pages I shall use this term to refer to a special kind of story about the past, one which symbolizes the values of a group and legitimates their position or claims. The question of the possible truth or falsehood of these stories will be left in suspense, except in cases when it is raised within the period under discussion.

---
[1] Eric J. Hobsbawm and Terence Ranger (eds.) *The Invention of Tradition* (Cambridge, 1983).

In the first place, family identities. Ruling dynasties like the Habsburgs and the Tudors encouraged the production of accounts of the past which emphasized the antiquity and the glorious deeds of their 'house'. In the case of the Tudors, one thinks of the claim to descent from King Arthur, after whom Henry VII named his eldest son (though Tudor pageants give King Arthur only a small role).[2] In the case of the Habsburgs, the heroic ancestors of the family were supposed to include Hercules and Jason, and Charles V's genealogy was traced back to Adam via Noah and Osiris.[3] Mere nobles were generally content with genealogies linking them to patrician families of ancient Rome with similar-sounding names, like the Venetian house of Cornaro to the Cornelii (Scipio's family), though a rival patrician family, the Giustinian, claimed descent from the emperor Justinian, and a patrician family from Ulm, the Rem, were credited with descent from Remus. For historians of mentalities, the question, What made these 'incredible genealogies' appear credible? is an important one.[4]

At a still more modest level, many new men commissioned genealogies which provided them with noble ancestors, however implausible these ancestors may have seemed. Two famous examples are those of Queen Elizabeth's minister William Cecil and Louis XIV's minister Jean-Baptiste Colbert. Cecil, of recent yeoman stock, was kitted out with a progenitor called 'Sitsylt', who fought in the Hundred Years' War, while Colbert, whose family were merchants from Rheims, was provided with noble ancestors from Scotland and even new funeral monuments to prove it.[5] The Medici, whose name was generally agreed to have come from a physician in the family, were no longer satisfied with this origin in the mid-sixteenth century. A Grand Duke needed something better, and a heroic ancestor by the name of

[2] Sydney Anglo, *Images of Tudor Kingship* (London, 1992), ch.2.
[3] Jan-Dirk Müller, *Gedachtnus* (Munich, 1982); Marie Tanner, *The Last Descendants of Aeneas: the Hapsburgs and the Mythic Image of the Emperor* (New Haven, 1993).
[4] Frank Borchardt, *German Antiquity in Renaissance Myth* (Baltimore MD, 1971), 105. Cf Colette Beaune, *The Birth of an Ideology* (1985: English translation, Berkeley CA, 1991), 63; Roberto Bizzocchi, *Genealogie incredibili: scritti di storia nell'Europa moderna* (Bologna, 1995).
[5] Jean Meyer, *Colbert* (Paris, 1981).

'Medix' was duly found.⁶ Even humanists could not resist this kind of fabrication, witness the Scaligers, of commoner origin, who connected themselves to the della Scala rulers of Verona.⁷

Other social groups also followed this practice – indeed, most corporations did so in the 'corporative state' of the old regime. Cities, for example, cultivated stories about their glorious origins. Londoners and Paduans claimed that their city was a 'New Troy' (the Paduan humanists declaring that the city had been founded by Antenor). Rome was the subject of a particularly rich mythology, of which the story of Romulus, Remus and the wolf was only a small part.⁸ Given the rivalry between cities is no surprise to discover that the claim to be a new Rome was made by Constantinople, Aachen, Trier, Milan and Reims (supposedly named after Remus) in the Middle Ages, and by Venice, Seville and Moscow in early modern times.⁹ The Florentines were attached to the story of their foundation in the time of the Roman Republic, a story which was taken as a guarantee of their liberty. The Venetians also had their myth of liberty, going back to the time when the city was founded in the water as a refuge from the barbarian invaders of Italy.¹⁰

Urban institutions such as craft guilds also made claims to antiquity and associated themselves with saints and other heroes who were treated as colleagues or founders as well as patrons (e.g. goldsmiths and St Eloi, shoemakers and St Crispin). Assemblies, the English Parliament for instance, were concerned with their own antiquity. In the 17th century, it was believed

---

[6] Henk van Veen, 'Art and Propaganda in Late Renaissance and Baroque Florence: the Defeat of Radagisus King of the Goths', *Journal of the Warburg and Courtauld Institutes* 47 (1984), 106-118.
[7] Anthony Grafton, *Joseph Scaliger* (Oxford, 1993), vol. 2, 76-82.
[8] Philip Jacks, *The Antiquarian and the Myth of Antiquity: the Origins of Rome in Renaissance Thought* (Cambridge, 1993). Cf Beaune, *Birth*, 70.
[9] David S. Chambers, *The Imperial Age of Venice* (London, 1971); Vicente Lleó Cañal, *Nueva Roma: mitología y humanismo en el renacimiento sevillano* (Seville, 1979); Hildegard Schaeder, *Moskau das dritte Rom* (1929: reprinted Darmstadt, 1957).
[10] Donald Weinstein, 'The Myth of Florence', in *Florentine Studies*, ed. Nicolai Rubinstein (London, 1970), 15-44; Franco Gaeta, 'Alcune considerazioni sul mito di Venezia', *Bibliothèque d'humanisme et Renaissance* 23 (1961), 58-75; William Bouwsma, *Venice and the Defense of Republican Liberty* (Berkeley CA, 1968).

that Parliament was an Anglo-Saxon or 'Gothic' institution.[11] The French *parlements* went one better by deriving themselves from annual meetings of the 'senate' of the Druids.[12] Universities liked to claim distant origins: Bologna claimed on the basis of a forged document to have been founded by the emperor Theodosius in 423, while Oxford and Cambridge were supposed to have been founded by King Arthur and King Alfred.

In some countries, the nobility, a legally-privileged estate or order, claimed to have a different origin from ordinary people. The French nobles claimed that they were descended from the Franks, the conquerors, while the peasants were descended from the Gauls, a subject people.[13] They also claimed that they were descended from Noah's son Japhet, while the peasants were defended from Cam (Ham), a historical legitimation of noble racism, the myth of blue blood so common in early modern Europe. Alternatively, they claimed that commoners were descended from Noah's servants or even from Cain. 'La noblesse est issue d'Abel et des enfants de Noé, les plébeiens de Cain et des serviteurs de Noé sortis de l'arche'.[14]

The Church contributed to this process of myth-making with its stories of saints, some of whom were the patrons of local or national communities. We should add stories about religious orders (the Carmelite friars, for instance, claimed to have been founded long before Christ, by the prophet Elijah). There were also accounts of the Church's own history, including the famous 'Donation of Constantine'. In the late Middle Ages and the Renaissance, the papacy justified its claim to the Papal States on the grounds that the emperor Constantine had given this territory to pope Sylvester and his successors, in gratitude for being cured of leprosy and converted to Christianity.[15].

---

[11] Samuel Kliger, *The Goths in England* (Cambridge MA, 1952), 7-8.
[12] Beaune, *Birth*.
[13] François Hotman, *Franco-Gallia* (1576: ed. Ralph E. Giesey, Cambridge 1972).
[14] Stanisław Cynarski, 'The Shape of Sarmatian Ideology in Poland', *Acta Poloniae Historia* 19 (1968), 5-17; Arlette Jouanna, *Ordre Social* (Paris 1978), 68; Jean de Saulx-Tavannes, quoted in André Devyver, *Le sang épuré* (Brussels, 1973), 177.
[15] Christopher B. Coleman (ed.) *The Donation of Constantine* (New Haven, 1922).

However, the Catholic Church being an international organization, it had little to do with some of the most famous early modern myths, which concerned the origin and destiny of peoples or nations.[16] For national consciousness of a kind existed long before the rise of nationalism and the nation-state in the nineteenth century – the main difference being that early modern discussions of nationhood had little to say about, or to, ordinary people.[17]

One important model for these myths was the story of the people of Israel. The theme of the holy land, the chosen people or the elect nation was a recurrent one, in the case of medieval France, for instance.[18] It can be found in Renaissance Florence, especially in the age of the prophet Savonarola, who saw Florence as a New Jerusalem.[19] It can be found in Tudor England, described in Foxe's *Book of Martyrs*, one of the most-read books of the time, as an 'elect nation'.[20] It was a central part of the self-image of the new Dutch Republic which came into existence in the late sixteenth century.[21] The later American sense of 'manifest destiny' may be viewed as a semi-secularized version of the idea of the elect nation.[22]

In the search for collective identity and for ways of expressing it, a second model was the story of the Trojans. It was claimed that the French royal family, for instance, were descended from Francus the Trojan, founder of France.[23] In similar fashion Britain

---

[16] Anthony D. Smith, *The Ethnic Origins of Nations* (London, 1986).
[17] Contrast Eugen Weber, *Peasants into Frenchmen* (Stanford CA, 1974) and Beaune, *Birth*.
[18] Joseph Strayer 'France: the Holy Land, the Chosen People, and the Most Christian King', in Theodore K. Rabb and Jerrold Seigel (eds.) *Action and Conviction in Early Modern Europe* (Princeton NJ, 1969), 3-16.
[19] Weinstein, *Myth*; Lorenzo Polizzotto, *The Elect Nation: the Savonarolan Movement in Florence* (Oxford, 1994).
[20] William Haller, *Foxe's Book of Martyrs and the Elect Nation* (London, 1963).
[21] G. Groenhuis, 'Calvinism and National Consciousness: the Dutch Republic as the New Israel', in Alistair C. Duke and Coen A. Tamse (eds.) *Too Mighty to be Free: censorship and the press in Britain and the Netherlands* (Zutphen, 1981), 118-33; Simon Schama, *The Embarrassment of Riches* (London, 1987).
[22] Ernest Tuveson, *The Redeemer Nation: the Idea of America's Millennial Role* (Chicago IL, 1968).
[23] Jean Lemaire des Belges, *Les illustrations de Gaule et singularités de Troye* (1509: ed. J. Stecher, reprinted Geneva 1969), cf Claude- Gilbert Dubois, *Celtes et Gaulois au 16e siècle* (Paris, 1972), 31-9; Pierre Ronsard, *Franciade* (1572: ed. Isidore Silver, Chicago IL 1966); Beaune, *Birth*.

was supposed to have been founded by Brutus the Trojan. Some Venetians told a similar story.[24] Readers may be surprised at this cult of the losers and at the absence of descent from the Greeks. The point was, however, that the Romans claimed descent from Aeneas and his Trojan companions, and that early modern Europeans, until the later 18th century, admired ancient Rome more than ancient Greece.

Other peoples gave themselves more exotic ancestors, or more exactly were furnished with these ancestors by humanists. The Scots, for example, trumped the English claims to be Trojans by the claim to be descended from Scota, daughter of one of the Pharaohs.[25] Europeans who had not been not incorporated into the Roman empire, and even some who were, tended to identify with peoples the Romans regarded as barbarians. The Czechs claimed descent from a certain Czechus, who came from the East with his brother Lech.[26] The Swedes claimed descent from the Goths (as bishop Ragvald did at the Council of Basel in 1434), and as a result there was a cult of the Goths in sixteenth- and seventeenth-century Sweden. As Gustav II Adolf reminded the Riksdag in 1630, the Swedish nobility were 'the true heirs and descendants of the ancient Goths, who in their day conquered almost the whole earth'.[27] The Spaniards identified themselves with the Visigoths who had invaded the Iberian peninsula.[28] Some of the French and the Germans emphasized their Celtic origins and developed a cult of the Druids.[29] The Tuscans claimed to be the Etruscans.[30] The Poles claimed descent from the Sarmatians, and the Hungarians from the Huns (hence to this day 'Attila' is

---

[24] Edward Muir, *Civic Ritual in Renaissance Venice* (Princeton NJ, 1981).
[25] William Matthews, 'The Egyptians in Scotland: the Political History of a Myth', *Viator* 1 (1970), 289-306.
[26] Bizzocchi, *Genealogie*, 232f.
[27] Johannes Nordström, *De yoerbornes ö* (Stockholm, 1934); Kurt Johannesson, *The Renaissance of the Goths in 16th-Century Sweden* (Berkeley CA, 1991).
[28] Johannes Nordström, 'Goter och Spanjorer', *Lychnos* (1944-45), 257-80 and (1971-72), 171-80.
[29] George Huppert, 'The Trojan Franks and their Critics', *Studies in the Renaissance* 12, 227-41; id., *The Idea of Perfect History* (Urbana IL, 1970), ch. 4; Dubois, *Celtes*; Beaune, *Birth*; Borchardt, *German Antiquity*.
[30] Giovanni Cipriani, *Il mito etrusco nel rinascimento fiorentino* (Florence, 1980).

a popular first name for Hungarian boys). The Dutch identified themselves with the Batavians who resisted the Roman Empire's attempt to deprive them of their liberty, re-enacting this resistance in their 80 year's war with Spain.[31]

For some scholars, at least, even these genealogies did not go back far enough. Some indeed claimed that their language was the world's original language, spoken in the Garden of Eden. These claims were made for German, for example; for Dutch, in a book by the Antwerp humanist Johannes Goropius; and for Swedish, in a study by Olaus Rudbeckius.[32]

Europe was also mythologized. The story of Europa and the bull was known and retold in this period. Distinctions between the three continents were explained and legitimated by means of the story of the three sons of Noah, Japhet being the ancestor of Europeans, Sem of Asians and Cham of Africans.[33] However, myths of Europe were given much less prominence than myths of nations, perhaps because the sense of being European was less widespread and less deep than that of belonging to a national group.

From a functional anthropologist's point of view, one might regard the stories of Jesus and the early Church as so many myths legitimating the existence of the unit 'Christendom'. In this period, however, despite the increasing awareness of other cultures, Christians do not seem to have felt much need to justify their existence. What one does find, on the other hand, are stories legitimating or de-legitimating the Reformation, or origin myths of national churches. In the time of Queen Elizabeth, for example, an archbishop of Canterbury, the scholar Matthew Parker, claimed that the Church of England had been founded not by Rome but by a special visit to the island on the part of Joseph of Arimathea.

There are three obvious questions which need to be asked about this corpus of narratives, images and rituals. In the first place, the question of the public, the consumers, the

---
[31] Henri van de Waal, *Drie eeuwen vaderlandsche geschieduitbeelding* (The Hague, 1952); Schama, *Embarrassment*, 76-81.
[32] Arnold Borst, *Der Turmbau von Babel*, Stuttgart (1957-63), vol. 3, 1215-19.
[33] Denys Hay, *Europe: the emergence of an idea* (Edinburgh, 1957).

communities of interpretation and the boundaries between them. They are difficult boundaries to draw. It is indeed possible that the problem of national origins was a subject of interest only to humanists and their princely or noble patrons with their galleries of ancestors and their funeral monuments (for example the grand monument to the emperor Maximilian at Innsbruck). However, the possibility of a wider audience is implied by the illustration of some of these myths in paintings displayed in public and still more important, their re-enactment in public rituals like the Wedding of the Sea in Venice, the Lord Mayor's Shows in London, royal entries in Paris, and so on.[34]

Accounts of these rituals reveal the importance of the past in the early modern present, as vivid as in the 20th-century American town described by the anthropologist W. L. Warner in his fine but unjustly neglected book on Memorial Day.[35] Unfortunately, there is little evidence about the reaction of ordinary people to these shows, and still less about their interest in, or interpretation of, myths of national or urban origin.

The second and possibly the most difficult question is that of the status of the stories. It is the kind of question posed and brilliantly explored by Paul Veyne in his essay, *Did the ancient Greeks believe in their myths*? His conclusion, about the need to distinguish different senses of 'believe', is I think valid in this case too.[36] I have used the term 'cult' more than once in this chapter, and it should be emphasized that the stories of origins discussed here had a special, quasi-sacred status. To question them was to break a taboo, as is clear from the violent reactions to criticisms of their authenticity, by Polydore Vergil, for example, an Italian humanist who dared to deny the Trojan origins of the British and even the existence of King Arthur. A number of British scholars (Bale, for instance, Leland, Lhuyd, Savile and

---

[34] Sydney Anglo (1969) *Spectacle, Pageantry and Early Tudor Policy* (Oxford, 1969); David Bergeron, *English Civic Pageantry* (Columbia SC, 1971); Frances Yates, *Astraea* (London, 1975), 127-48; Beaune, *Birth*.
[35] Muir, *Civic Ritual*; Cf Warner, *The Living*.
[36] Veyne, *Did the Greeks Believe*?

Neville), found this revisionism impossible to accept.[37] As late as 1714, a French scholar was sent to the Bastille for asserting the German rather than the Trojan origins of the Franks (an implicit criticism of absolute monarchy, since early Germany was associated with liberty).[38]

Other people liked the myths but did not take them so literally. The poet Ronsard, for example, author of the *Franciade* (1572) and epic poem on the origins of France modelled on Virgil's *Aeneid*. In the preface to this poem, Ronsard says he used the old story of Francus without worrying whether or not it was true ('sans me soucier si cela est vrai ou non, ou si nos rois sont Troyens ou Germains... si Francus est venu en France ou non').[39]

The third and last question concerns the purposes, uses or functions of these stories. Here I should like to begin by invoking the shade of Bronisław Malinowski and especially his idea of myth as charter. To invoke Malinowski here and now may seem odd, for two reasons. In the first place, there is a kind of circular tour involved, since Malinowski presumably used the term 'charter' with reference to Magna Carta, and the interpretation of Magna Carta in the seventeenth century in particular is a classic case of a story about the past being reinterpreted in order to justify institutions in the present. A document which was essentially concerned with thirteenth-century problems like fish-weirs on the Thames was used in order to support arguments in favour of *habeas corpus*, the privileges of parliament, and so on.[40] Myths with a similar purpose included the 'ancient constitution', 'Gothic liberty' in England, Sweden, Spain and elsewhere, stories of the defence of liberty by the Batavians and Venetians, and the myth of the 'Norman Yoke' (in this case not

---

[37] Denys Hay, *Polydore Vergil* (Oxford, 1952); Fritz Levy, *Tudor Historical Thought* (San Marino, 1967), 130-142; May Mc Kisack, *Medieval History in the Tudor Age* (Oxford, 1971).
[38] George Huppert, The Trojan Franks and their Critics', *Studies in the Renaissance* 12 (1965), 227-41; id., *The Idea of Perfect History* (Urbana IL, 1970); Blondine Barret-Kriegel, *Jean Mabillon* (1988), 201-6.
[39] Pierre Ronsard, *Franciade* (1572: quoted in Yates, *Astraea*, 132.
[40] Faith Thompson, *Magna Carta: its Role in the Making of the English Constitution*, 1300-1629 (Minneapolis MN, 1948); Christopher Hill, *Intellectual Origins of the English Revolution* (Oxford, 1965), 152-3, 233-4, 245-6, 257-8.

a charter of the present but the reverse, a claim to lost rights).[41]

It would surely be mistaken to attempt to explain early modern myths in functionalist terms alone, but it is equally mistaken to reject functionalist explanations altogether. Take the case of the Donation of Constantine. The story was told and retold in order to legitimate a claim by the popes that was challenged in the fifteenth and still more in the sixteenth century. In similar fashion, English Protestants used the story of the visit of Joseph of Arimathea to show that their church had been independent of Rome from the beginning.

However, the examples offered here have illustrated the place of the past not only in the legitimation but also in the definition, perhaps the construction, of collective identities of various kinds. If the original impulse to the creation of these stories was often utilitarian, the debates which followed raised broader issues and encouraged a wider interest in the early medieval and even in the prehistoric past, witness, for instance, the engravings of runes and barrows illustrating the history of Sweden written by the seventeenth-century scholar Olof Rudbeck.

This analysis of the myths of early modern Europeans is not intended to suggest that their successors, ourselves included, have gone beyond myth. We still tell stories in order to justify ourselves and our institutions. This point is recognized by students of nationalism. The sociologist Anthony Smith, for instance, in a study of the ethnic origins of nations, speaks of a 'myth-symbol complex', a 'constitutive myth', or a *mythomoteur* (a term he borrows from the Catalan scholar Ramon d'Abadal i de Vinyals). If a nation is an 'imagined community', in Benedict Anderson's famous phrase, then narratives of its origins or its past in general will obviously help to hold it together.[42]

If this is the case, an important question is waiting to be

---

[41] Nordström, *De yoerbornes ö*; Kliger, *Goths*; Christopher Hill, 'The Norman Yoke', *Puritanism and Revolution* (London, 1958), 50-122; John Pocock, *The Ancient Constitution and the Feudal Law* (1957: second edn. Cambridge 1987), especially 16-19.

[42] Smith, *Ethnic Origins*, esp. 58-68; Benedict Anderson, *Imagined Communities: Reflections on the Origin and Spread of Nationalism* (1983: second edition London 1991); Homi Bhabha (ed.,) *Nation and Narration* (London, 1991).

asked. It is generally believed that Europeans today live in a very different intellectual world from that of their medieval and early modern ancestors, whether the shift from one to the other is viewed as sudden or gradual, whether the frontier between the world is located around 1800 or around 1650, whether the change is supposed to affect everyone or only the elites. Admitting that some kind of myth is necessary for every human community, large or small, it still makes sense to ask whether new myths are different from old ones, whether the essential plot has changed. One possible difference is the role of the hero. Heroes have certainly not disappeared from the cultural or political scene, but it would be surprising to find the Czechs, say, appealing to a founder such as 'Czechus' in order to distinguish themselves from the Slovaks. Today, they are more likely to appeal to collective cultural traditions, rather than to origins or to an individual.

Another point which must be taken into account in any analysis of modern myths is the rise of historical criticism, which is so much more widely known than it was in the sixteenth and seventeenth centuries. Telling stories about the past is therefore a more self-conscious activity than it used to be. For better or worse, traditions cannot be taken for granted, because there are many Polydore Vergils at work today, especially in universities, and genealogies of various kinds have become incredible. So what happens? To answer this question even in a provisionally satisfactory way would require another chapter, if not a book or a series of volumes, so I shall do no more than offer a single example, hopefully a case study with wider implications.

Charles V has already made his appearance in these pages as a descendant of Noah, Osiris and Hercules. Charles was mythologized in other ways in his own day, partly in order to construct that community of communities known as the Habsburg Empire. In the seventeenth and eighteenth centuries, although the emperor was discussed in a cool and critical manner in some countries, from France to Scotland, he continued to be presented as a heroic figure in the lands of both the Spanish and the Austrian Habsburgs. Charles VI in particular appealed to glorious memories of his ancestor and namesake in his own public self-presentation.

In the nineteenth and early twentieth centuries, however, the image of Charles changed. To some extent this was the result of the rise of document-based Rankean history, which presented the emperor as a fallible human being who did not take all the decisions made in his name. However, Charles was also remythologized. At a time of the construction or reconstruction of national communities, German historians described him as essentially German, Spaniards as essentially Spanish, while Belgian historians were convinced that the emperor was Belgian at heart.

In the middle of the twentieth century, his image changed again. Charles became the 'father' or the 'ancestor' of a broader community known as 'Europe', doubtless chosen, like his supposed ancestor Charlemagne, because the domains of these two emperors largely coincided with the territory of the Common Market. In a speech delivered on 3 July 1962, Charles De Gaulle described European Union as a dream of Charles V's. The five hundredth anniversary of the emperor's birth occurred in the year 2000, and was marked by commemorative volumes in Brussels and Madrid. Genealogy or legitimation by descent still seems to matter, even if the nature of the descent has changed. In the sixteenth century, Charles's descent from Hercules was taken literally, whether it was accepted or rejected. Today, Charles is presented as a symbol of a European community, as part of its cultural 'heritage'.

4: Myths of Venice

This chapter is concerned with images of Venice, visual, literary and occasionally musical. In the last half-century, specialists on Venice have come to adopt the term 'the myth of Venice' to refer in particular to the idea that the early modern city was the capital of an unusually free, tolerant and harmonious state (Fasoli 1958, Gaeta 1961). Discussing the culture as well as the polity, I shall use the term 'myths of Venice' in the plural, noting that they are like most myths in the sense of presenting their protagonist as larger than life, but unlike most myths because the hero is collective not individual.

Venetian culture, unlike that of Florence, has traditionally been suspicious of outstanding individuals. Instead, we find the glorification of a place, 'The Paradise of cities', as Ruskin called it (quoted in Norwich 2003, 72: cf. Clegg, 1981). The city was glorified by the Venetians themselves as well as by foreigners, in orations, travelogues, poems, plays, novels, paintings, films and operas. Venice was the setting of a number of operas, including Gioacchino Rossini's *Otello* (1816), Gaetano Donizetti's *Marino Faliero* (1835), Giuseppe Verdi's *I Due Foscari* (1844), Amilcare Ponchielli's *La Gioconda* (1876) and Benjamin Britten's *Death in Venice* (1973).

To limit this large topic, my concern here will be not so much with the individual reactions of major writers or artists as with what might be called the place of Venice in the European imagination – leaving others to investigate how the Arabs (say) or the Japanese view or read the city, treating it as a text and 'scripting' it. In other words, I shall concentrate on *topoi*, producing a composite or collective image, literary or visual, a conducted tour of common places.

The aim, then, is a kind of collage, or better, perhaps, a Venetian mosaic. However, what follows cannot take the form of a simple mosaic, for several different reasons. In the first place, the images are not clearly separated; they merge or flow into one another. Again, northerners and southerners, Catholics and Protestants, males and females, and, not least, insiders and outsiders viewed the city in different ways. Yet again, in the hands of skilled writers and artists it is possible to see many variations on stock themes, which are elaborated developed or played with, leading to surprising twists and turns of the kind we so often find in the *calli* of the city itself.

Some writers and artists made a considerable impact on their readers and viewers, in other words on the collective imagination. In Venice, even more than in most other cities one has the sense of visitors following in the footsteps of others and seeing through the eyes of others, whether they realize this or not. Some of these travellers apparently believe that they are the first to make a common observation, but others are aware of what we call 'intertextuality' and quote or comment on their predecessors.

Among the more self-conscious visitors was Mrs Hester Piozzi, who declared that, thanks to Canaletto, her party could recognize 'all the famous towers, steeples etc' in Venice 'before we reached them' (Pfister 1996, 242). Turner too was indebted to 'Canaletti', as he calls him. Ruskin remarked that 'My Venice, like Turner's, had been chiefly created for us by Byron' (Pfister, 1996, 350). Robert Browning, Henry James, Marcel Proust – not to mention his character 'Marcel' – all took Ruskin's book with them and saw the stones of Venice in a Ruskinian light. Some nineteenth-century English tourists saw the Rialto Bridge through the eyes of Shakespeare or Thomas Otway, despite the

Myths of Venice

fact that neither of these playwrights is recorded ever to have visited the city (McPherson, 1990).

What follows will concentrate on the successive dominance of three images, the political image that stressed harmony and liberty and was dominant in the sixteenth and seventeenth centuries; then the hedonist image of a city of pleasure, most common in the eighteenth century, and finally, from the nineteenth century onwards, the aesthetic image of decaying beauty or beautiful decay. In the first phase, outsiders seem to have accepted the Venetians' self-image, but after the year 1700 or so the reverse was the case and the view from outside became dominant, even if it was and is not accepted by everyone.

I

The first myth of Venice was a story about the past that justified the political system; a story in which the characters were stereotyped, with idealized images of the Venetians contrasted with negative stereotypes of others, such as Byzantines or Turks. The myth emphasized certain key dates in the city's history such as the years 421 (the foundation), 828 (the arrival of the relics of St Mark), and 1177 (when Venice made peace between the empire and the papacy). Venice was presented as a New Rome, from the fifteenth-century humanists to the Welshman James Howell, who published a book about Venice in 1651 under the title *SPQV* (Marx 1978). Its constitution was supposed to combine monarchy, aristocracy and democracy and was supposed to ensure political harmony, longevity and above all, liberty (Fasoli 1958, Gaeta 1961, Gilmore 1973, Blythe 1992).

Thus the patrician Marin Sanudo wrote in the 1490s of 'a free land never subjugated by anyone like all others' (quoted in Brown, 511). Venetian ambassadors to the Ottoman Empire defined it by contrast to their own regime, using words like 'despotic' (Valensi, 1987). Venetian liberty was linked to the origins of the city, celebrated in 1421, a commemoration of a millennium at a time when even centenaries were still rare events.

Foreigners came to accept the Venetian view of themselves. The most eloquent description of Venetian liberty (at least of the negative aspect of liberty, 'freedom from') comes from the pen of the Welshman William Thomas, who wrote in the 1540s that:

> No man there marketh another's doings or ... meddleth with another man's living ... No man shall ask thee why thou comest not to church ... to live married or unmarried, no man shall ask thee why. For eating of flesh in thine own house, what day soever it be, it maketh no matter (Thomas 1963, 83)

Thomas came from rural Wales and it is difficult to avoid the thought that this passage says something in reverse about the world in which he grew up.

The central theme of Thomas Otway's play *Venice Preserved* (1682) is liberty, explicitly in Venice in the early seventeenth century at the time of the Spanish conspiracy against the city's independence and implicitly in England following the recent collective fears of a 'Popish Plot' (Mackenney, 2000). At the other end of Europe, the Poles, proud of the liberty they enjoyed in their 'commonwealth' (*Rzeczpospolita*), in which the power of the ruler was limited, liked to compare the king with the doge and their system of government with that of Venice (Kostylo, 2006).

Hostile images of Venice were also current in early modern Europe, as indeed they still are in different forms, reacting against the tourist city. There was an 'anti-myth' as well as a myth of Venice, a black legend as well as a golden one, viewing the city as a dystopia rather than a utopia, hell in place of paradise, and emphasising despotism rather than liberty and conflict and conspiracy rather than harmony.

Expressions of this view can already be found in the seventeenth century, notably in the anonymous *Squitinio della libertá veneta* (*Scrutiny of Venetian Liberty*, 1612); the demystifying *Histoire du gouvernement de Venise* (1676) by the Frenchman Abraham Nicolas Amelot de la Houssaye; and a text falsely attributed to the pro-Venetian friar Paolo Sarpi, *Opinione come debba governarsi ... Venezia* (1681). This pejorative view of republican Venice became especially common after the end of the Republic in 1797 (Wootton 1994, Infelise 1999).

Two French-speaking historians of the early nineteenth century, Jean Charles Léonard de Sismondi, in his *Histoire des republiques italiennes du moyen age* (1807-1818) and Pierre Daru, in his *Histoire de la République de Venise* (1817-1819) turned the Venetian concept of despotism against the Republic itself, presenting Venice as secretive and as a tyranny ruled by the Council of Ten. This 'Black Legend' emphasized the Venetian police state, including informers and assassinations, and took its most vivid form in the stories about Venetian prisons (the notorious *piombi* and *pozzi*). Ponchielli's opera, set in the seventeenth century and adapting a play by Victor Hugo, emphasizes the role of the spies of the Inquisition and the 'lion's mouth' letter-box in which secret denunciations could be posted.

Part at least of this 'Black Legend' was accepted by Venetians themselves, or at least by some guides to the tourists who recorded it in their journals. To quote the poet Samuel Rogers, who visited Venice in 1814,

> Saw also the chamber of the Council of Ten, into which the state-prisoners were brought up for examination from the *piombi* or the *pozzi* ... the closet lined with a black wainscot in which he [the prisoner] received his sentence of death, before he was led ... across the Ponte de' Sospiri to be strangled in the first dungeon on the left')Rogers 1956, 174-5).

(the last phrase suggests that the information came from a guide). Charles Dickens, who visited the city in 1844, was also impressed by the stories of strangling prisoners and of sinking the bodies in the lagoons (Dickens 1846, chapter 7). As a relief from darkness and dungeons we may turn to the hedonist image of the city.

II

Pleasure and sex have long been associated with Venice. Liberty was linked to licence. The city was famous or notorious for its courtesans, so that a brothel in Elizabethan London was called 'Venice'. In the sixteenth and seventeenth centuries, this association was generally evoked in a disapproving way. Long before Byron, Venice was described as a new Sodom by a fifteenth-century Florentine poet.

Such an image of Venice helps us to interpret vaguer noises of disapproval. The French poet Clément Marot, who was sympathetic to Protestantism by the time of his visit to Venice in 1536, described the Venetians as epicureans: 'Ils sont vivans à la loi d'Epicure' (Marot 1958, xliii).The English gentleman Fynes Moryson described the patricians of Venice as 'trained up in pleasure and wantonness', while Rogers called the Venetians 'the most sensual and luxurious people for many ages' (Moryson 1617, 90; Rogers 1956, 173).

In other writers – or sometimes the same ones – we find a positive view of the city of pleasure, the *città galante*, what Virginia Woolf would later call a 'playground' (quoted in Pemble 1995, 109). In its article 'Venise', the *Encyclopédie*, for instance, emphasized 'les plaisirs'. These pleasures included not only sex but also Carnival and gambling at the *ridotto*. Byron, who visited the city in 1816, described Venice in *Childe Harold* as 'the pleasant place of all festivity/the revels of the earth, the Masque of Italy' (quoted in Wilson 1974). The visual equivalent of Byron is a painting by William Etty entitled *Window in Venice, during a Festa*, exhibited in 1831, showing a balcony and three young women, one of whom reveals her breasts.

Despite these alternatives, sexual pleasures dominate the hedonist vision. The city was associated with Giacomo Casanova, who declared in his autobiography that his aim in life was 'to cultivate the pleasures of the senses'. This eighteenth-century view of Venice would be revived and reconstructed in the late nineteenth century, the age of the aesthetes. The young Hugo von Hofmannsthal was deeply impressed by Venice in general and the memoirs of Casanova in particular, and the two together inspired a number of his works (Bianquis 1958, Pemble 1995, 108).

The idea of Venice itself as an object of desire – the city as a woman – is a recurrent one (Tanner 1992). In Otway's play *Venice Preserved* (1682) one character, Pierre, calls the city itself 'The Adriatic whore'. Usually, the metaphor is positive. Venice is personified as a beautiful, majestic woman in the paintings of Tintoretto. Venice was associated with Venus in sixteenth-century poems. For the seventeenth-century Venetian poet Giovanni Francesco Busenello, the city was 'The queen of the sea, the goddess of the waves' (*La regina del mar, la dea dell'onde*). For the English poet John Ford, it was the 'Queen of cities'.

This image became an increasingly common one in the writings of foreign visitors in the nineteenth century, so much so that we might speak of the 'feminization' of the city. Byron described Venice as a goddess or 'the Ocean queen', while Wordsworth wrote of 'A maiden city'. Henry James elaborated the image, remarking that 'the creature varies like a woman, whom you know only when you know all the aspects of her beauty'. Proust went further still in describing Marcel's desire for Venice, the rivalry in his mind between Venice and Albertine, and the associations between the two.

Lesser writers also played variations on this theme. The American novelist Francis Marion Crawford described Venice as 'a woman of divine beauty, yet almost tragically jealous of her own freedom'. The French symbolist poet Henri de Régnier called the city 'la belle assiégée'. The most striking instance of feminization is perhaps the English travel writer Edward Hutton's description of Venice as 'thinking of her husband the sea', thus inverting the genders of the protagonists of the annual wedding ritual (Pemble 1995, 103, 114, 184).

III

Let us turn to the aesthetic image of the city. Venice first attracted crowds of visitors in the late Middle Ages, mainly pilgrims on the way to the Holy Land, because it was a treasury of relics. Later it became an aesthetic shrine, a treasury of works of art, even if a somewhat depleted one, since fragments of palaces were taken away and re-erected in Boston, New York and elsewhere, poetic justice for the Venetian despoiling of Constantinople in 1204, when the four great bronze horses, among other items of booty, were brought to St Mark's.

The Renaissance topos of Venetian colour as the rival of Florentine design was echoed by later visitors such as Etty who called the city 'the birthplace and cradle of colour'. At a time when Venetian painters were no longer famous, the Biennale, founded in 1895, linked Venice with the arts.

In any case, from about 1800 onwards the city itself was increasingly viewed as a sort of open-air museum or a work of art in itself. It was visited by many foreign painters: Bonington and Turner, Corot and Monet, Sickert and Sargent. It was viewed by tourists as 'picturesque'. By the late nineteenth century ordinary Venetians as well as the buildings were coming to be seen as picturesque, the subject of genre paintings by artists such as Cecil van Haanen (who painted bead-stringers), or James Whistler (who drew beggars and a fishmonger and claimed to have found 'A Venice in Venice, that the others seem never to have perceived'), or John Singer Sargent (who painted women drawing water from a well in a small *campo*). Local artists such as Giacomo Favretto (1849-1887), who painted street musicians, followed the trend (Honour and Fleming 1991; Grieve 2000).

In this aesthetic vision one recurrent theme is the idea of what Rogers called 'the city in the sea'. The Gothic novelist Ann Radcliffe wrote of palaces 'rising out of the sea', Byron of 'that sea-born city', Ruskin of the 'amphibious city'. Elaborating the idea, and perhaps inspired by the coral-coloured brick, Herman

Melville wrote about 'reefs of palaces'. Charles Dickens, Hans Christian Andersen and Henry James all viewed Venice as a ship, James describing Riva degli Schiavoni as the 'promenade-deck' (Honour and Fleming, 1991; Perosa, 1995).

A second major theme in what we might call 'the *flâneur*'s Venice' of the nineteenth century is that of decay and death, viewed with a kind of pleasurable melancholy. Byron declared that he did 'not even dislike the evident decay of the city', with its 'crumbling' palaces. Wordsworth described Venice as a 'shade' of its former self, and Ruskin, rather more poetically, called it 'a ghost upon the sands of the sea'. Shelley described the gondola as a 'funereal bark', Mark Twain compared it to a 'hearse', and Wagner complained that it made him feel he was 'taking part in a funeral procession during a pestilence', while some classically educated tourists saw the gondolier as Charon. Henry James viewed the whole city as a 'tomb' or a 'mausoleum'. In short, Mann's *Death in Venice*, despite its *fin-de-siècle* atmosphere, built on a longer tradition, as well as stimulating the famous adaptations by Luchino Visconti and Benjamin Britten.

A third aesthetic theme in the writings of visitors from the late eighteenth century onwards is that of the exotic and especially the oriental city, offering many vivid examples of the orientalism described and condemned by Edward Said (1978). William Beckford, who was there in 1782, fancied himself 'in the bazaars of Constantinople'. Rogers noticed the 'Saracenic' windows on the Grand Canal (Rogers 1956, 174). George Sand commented on the city's 'air de sultane'. When he saw San Marco, Melville thought it was 'as if the Grand Turk had pitched his pavilion here' (quoted in Tanner, 1992, 8). Ruskin wrote about Venice as the site of 'the meeting of the influences of the Eastern and Western races'. Henry James made the hero of his story 'Travelling Companions' (1870) declare on arrival in Venice that: 'I had left Europe: I was in the East'. The Dutch writer Louis Couperus described St Mark's as a 'mosque' (Couperus 1953-7, vol.2, 802). Proust wrote of 'tiny moorish windows' and 'Venetian palaces hidden like sultan's wives behind a screen of pierced stone' (Collier 1989).

Indeed, Venice was often seen as a setting for the *Arabian Nights*, thus combining the orientalizing gaze with the sense that the city was not quite real. The most famous expression of this idea is surely that of Proust, who feels 'like a character in the Arabian Nights' wandering 'a labyrinth of alleys like those palaces in oriental tales'. But this passage is the reworking of a topos, whether the author was conscious of this or no. Before Proust, Couperus had described St Mark's as a harem, as if 'a sultan lived there with princesses'.Ruskin had made a similar point about St Mark's, 'Like a scene from the *Arabian Nights*'. Before Ruskin, the American writer James Fenimore Cooper already 'felt as transported to a scene in the *Arabian Nights*' (Cooper 1838).

The sense of an unreal city was also expressed by comparing Piazza San Marco, as Couperus did, to 'the dazzling decor of the third act of a great opera' (*het schitterend verblindende décor van de derde akte ener grote opera*). Comparisons with the theatre are of course commonplaces of travel writing about other places too, whole countries such as Italy and Egypt as well as cities. Henry James once declared that 'to travel is, as it were, to go to the play' (James 1995, 82). The tourist gaze naturally produces what might be called the 'theatre effect'. All the same, some cities, Venice among them, lend themselves to this effect even more than others.

Venice might also be treated, in the words of Hester Piozzi, as an example of 'enchantment', of what the writer Elizabeth Eastlake called 'the witchery of Venice' and Whistler described as 'really a fairyland', while Couperus wrote – long before this phrase became fashionable – of 'the magic realism of its architecture' (*de magische werkelijkheid der architekturen*). It might be described as an 'Italian dream' (the title of Dickens's chapter on Venice), or 'dreamlike', as Ruskin did (Norwich 2003, 84), or as a 'dream' or 'mirage', like the poet Arthur Symons or, yet again, Louis Couperus on 'the dream of San Marco and the Doge's Palace' (*de droom van San Marco en het Dogen-paleis*). In similar fashion, Turner painted the city seen through a mist, in deliberate contrast to the sharp outlines of the townscapes of Canaletto and Guardi (Warrell 2003).

IV

The singularity of Venice is part of its self-image, part of the myth. Francesco Sansovino's *Venetia città nobilissima e singolare* dates from 1581, while a book published by the map-maker Vincenzo Coronelli in 1708-09 was entitled *Singolarità di Venezia*.

The question of singularity or exceptionalism is, paradoxically enough, a general one. Every city is different, but there are family resemblances between some cities and others.

Many cities have been personified as women, like Magdeburg during the Thirty Years' War. Genoa was another trading republic with a doge and senators. The much-vaunted liberty of Venice was shared or rivaled by Florence, Poland and the Swiss and Dutch Republics. A watery site is a feature of a number of other cities, Venices of the North such as Bruges, Amsterdam, Stockholm and St Petersburg, or American Venices such as Venezuela, Mexico City, Recife ('a Veneza brasileira') or Fort Lauderdale in Florida.

These names are at once a tribute to the singularity of Venice and an attempt to undermine it, like the attempts to replicate the city in Las Vegas and elsewhere. 'The Venetian' hotel in Vegas, which opened in 1999, reproduces not only paintings but Piazza San Marco itself (including the *campanile* but not the basilica) and the Rialto bridge, and offers trips by gondola down what is called 'the Grand Canal shopping complex'. In our age of globalization, Piazza San Marco has also been replicated in China: a 1.5 scale reconstruction in a theme park called 'Window of the World', opened in 1995 in the Shenzen zone; while a 'Venice' has also been constructed in Hangzhou. The city has also inspired 'Grand Venezia', described as a 'theme-based mall' in New Delhi.

Before we describe this combination of hotel and theme park as an instance of post-modernism – of Baudrillard's simulacrum, for instance – it is worth recalling that in London, at Olympia, a replica Venice opened as long ago as 1892 and served as the setting for a show performed twice daily, 'Venice the Bride of the Sea'(Pemble 1995, 177). Both simulacra and what is sometimes described as 'disneyfication' are older than we might think.

I have left to the last the special importance of Venice for the British. It may be illustrated by writers from Byron to Browning and painters from Turner to Sickert, as well as by Benjamin Britten. Today, as can be seen almost every year in the annual exhibition at the Royal Academy, Ken Howard carries on the pictorial tradition – indeed, in recent years Venice has contributed more townscapes to the Academy's exhibition than any other city but London. As for British historians of Venice, there are enough of them to form a society and found a newsletter, *News on the Rialto*.

This is surely a case of a perceived affinity, or even identification. The Fitzwilliam Museum in Cambridge owns an eighteenth-century painting of the Grand Canal juxtaposed to St Paul's. It is well known that members of the Whig party admired the Venetian constitution and wanted the king to be little more than a doge. However, the appeal of Venice was not limited to one position on the political spectrum. Howell's *SPQV* was published in 1651, two years after Charles I was beheaded, and it was dedicated to the Parliament. Otway, a Tory, implied a parallel between the Venetian crisis of the early seventeenth century and the English Exclusion Crisis of the later seventeenth century.[43]

John Ruskin's preface to his *Stones of Venice* (1851), published in the year of the Great Exhibition, introduced what he called 'a city which should surely be interesting to the men of London, as affording the richest existing example of architecture raised by a mercantile community, for civil uses, and domestic magnificence'. Ruskin also believed that Venice, like Carthage, had a political lesson to teach us. Remembering the fall of earlier maritime empires might help us avoid being 'led through prouder eminence to less pitied destruction'.

I doubt whether these imperial associations tell us much about the appeal of Venice for us today. I would place more emphasis on the absence of cars, making it easier for visitors to imagine themselves walking in the world of the Renaissance. But we still

---

[43] Mackenney, '"A Plot Discover'd?".

have to explain the special appeal of Venice to the British. Are we not drawn to Venice because the waters show us a sort of reflection of ourselves?

References

Geneviève Bianquis, 'L'image de Venise dans l'oeuvre de Hofmannsthal', *Revue de littérature comparée*, 32 (1958), 321-26.

James M. Blythe, *Ideal Government and Mixed Constitution in the Middle Ages* (Princeton NJ, 1992).

Patricia Fortini Brown, 'The Self-Definition of the Venetian Republic', in *City-States in Classical Antiquity and Medieval Italy*, ed. by Anthony Molho, Kurt Raaflaub and Julia Emlen (Stuttgart, 1991), 511-48.

Jeanne Clegg, *Ruskin and Venice* (London, 1981).

Peter Collier, *Proust and Venice* (Cambridge, 1989).

James Fenimore Cooper, *Excursions in Italy* (London, 1838).

Louis Couperus, *Verzamelde werken*, 12 vols. (Amsterdam, 1953-7).

Régis Debray, *Contre Venise* (Paris, 1995).

Charles Dickens, *Pictures from Italy* (London, 1846).

Gina Fasoli, 'Nascita di un mito' (1958; rpr. in her *Scritti di storia medievale* (Bologna, 1974), 445-72.

Franco Gaeta, 'Alcune considerazioni sul mito di Venezia', *Bibliothèque d'Humanisme & Renaissance* 23 (1961), 58-75.

Myron Gilmore, 'Myth and Reality in Venetian Political Theory', in *Renaissance Venice*, ed. by John R. Hale (London, 1973), 431-44.

Alastair Grieve, *Whistler's Venice* (New Haven CN, 2000).

Hugh Honour and John Fleming, *The Venetian Hours of Henry James, Whistler and Sargent* (London, 1991).

Mario Infelise, 'Intorno alla leggenda nera di Venezia nella prima metà dell'800', in *Venezia e l'Austria*, ed. by Gino Benzoni and Gaetano Cozzi (Venice, 1999), 309-21.

Henry James, *Italian Hours* (Harmondsworth, 1995), 82.

Joanna Kostylo, 'The Discourse of Republicanism in Early-modern Europe, with Special Reference to Venice and Poland', Ph.D. dissertation, Dept of Modern Languages, University of Cambridge, 2006.

Richard Mackenney, '"A Plot Discover'd?" Myth, Legend and the Spanish Conspiracy against Venice in 1618', in John Martin and Dennis Romano, eds., *Venice Reconsidered: The History and Civilization of an Italian City-state, 1297-1797* (Baltimore, 2000), 185-216.

Clément Marot, *Epitres*, ed. by Claude Albert Mayer (London, 1958)

Barbara Marx, *Venezia-altera Roma? Ipotesi sull'umanesimo veneziano* (Venice, 1978).

David C. McPherson, *Shakespeare, Jonson and the Myth of Venice* (Newark NJ, 1990).

Fynes Moryson, *Itinerary* (1617; facsimile edn Amsterdam, 1971).

John Julius Norwich, *The Paradise of Cities: Nineteenth-century Venice Seen through Foreign Eyes* (London, 2003).

John Pemble, *Venice Rediscovered* (Oxford, 1995).

Sergio Perosa (ed.) *Henry James e Venezia* (Florence, 1995).

Manfred Pfister, *The Fatal Gift of Beauty: The Italies of British Travellers: An Annotated Anthology* (Amsterdam, 1996).

Samuel Rogers, *Italian Journal*, ed. by John R. Hale (London: Faber, 1956).

Edward Said, *Orientalism* (London, 1978).

Tony Tanner, *Venice Desired* (Cambridge MA, 1992).

William Thomas, *The History of Italy*, ed. by George B. Parks (Ithaca NY, 1963).

Lucette Valensi, *The Birth of the Despot: Venice and the Sublime Porte* (1987: English trans. Ithaca NY, 1993).

Ian Warrell, *Turner and Venice* (London, 2003).

Milton Wilson, 'Traveller's Venice: Some Images from Byron and Shelley', *University of Toronto Quarterly*, 43 (1974), 93-120.

David Wootton, 'Ulysses Bound? Venice and the Idea of Liberty from Howell to Hume', in *Republicanism, Liberty, and Commercial Society, 1649-1776*, ed. by Wootton (Stanford CA, 1994), 341-67.

5: HISTORY, MYTH AND FICTION, DOUBTS AND DEBATES

For 'scientific' historians of the nineteenth and early twentieth centuries, the three central concepts around which this chapter is organized were obviously distinct. 'History' was a true story, 'fiction' an invented story presented as such, and 'myth' an invented story presented as a true one. Today, matters no longer seem so simple. We have learned that in different cultures and in different periods, the boundary between what we call 'history' and what we call 'fiction' has been drawn in different places as well as with different degrees of precision. It is therefore imperative to translate these concepts into the terms – themselves changing – that were employed in the four centuries under discussion.

In the Middle Ages, some writers made a distinction between 'history' and what they called 'fable' (*fabula*), while some chroniclers criticized others (as William of Newburgh criticized Geoffrey of Monmouth) for telling 'lies'. All the same, the boundary between history and fiction (whether in the cases of the lives of the saints, or the romances of Arthur and Charlemagne), was an extremely open one.[1] For medieval readers, texts that we might place on the 'fiction' side of the boundary, such as stories about the siege of Troy or King Arthur, were apparently works of history.

---

[1] Ruth Morse, *Truth and Convention in the Middle Ages* (Cambridge, 1991); Peter G. Bietenholz, *Historia and Fabula: Myths and Legends in Historical Thought from Antiquity to the Modern Age* (Leiden, 1994), 62-145.

The Renaissance and the Reformation

In the Renaissance, as in the Middle Ages, explicit distinctions between history and 'fable' were sometimes made. The invention of speeches and the fabrication of documents were denounced by some scholars. In his *Method* for understanding history, Jean Bodin criticized the Italian historian Paolo Giovio for these practices, while the translator Jacques Gohorry compared the work of Giovio to a romance of chivalry, *Amadís de Gaula*.

All the same, there were many instances of what now appear to be blatant transgressions of the boundary between history and fiction. Homer was still taken seriously as a historian. Following classical models, the invention of speeches placed in the mouths of ambassadors or commanders was a common practice in the historical works of humanist historians such as Leonardo Bruni, Poggio Bracciolini and Francesco Guicciardini.

Documents such as letters, treaties or decrees inserted into the text of a history might also be fabrications. In the Renaissance, as the Middle Ages, a number of texts were in circulation which turned out to be inauthentic: the correspondence between St Paul and the Roman philosopher Seneca, for instance, the treatises attributed to 'Dionysius the Areopagite' (a pagan philosopher with whom St Paul conversed in Athens); the so-called 'hermetic' writings attributed to the Egyptian sage Hermes Trismegistus; and the 'Donation of Constantine', a kind of charter conferring on Pope Sylvester and his successors the lands later known as the States of the Church. Secular texts included two accounts of the Trojan War from rival points of view, attributed to Dares the Phrygian and Dictys the Cretan and believed to be older than Homer.

New forgeries were added during the Renaissance, among them the texts attributed to the ancient Babylonian writer 'Berosus' but actually produced by a sixteenth-century Italian friar, Annius of Viterbo, and the so-called 'lead books' discovered in Granada in 1588.[2] These texts were usually intended to justify

---

[2] Anthony Grafton, *Defenders of the Text* (Princeton, 1991), 76-103; Julio Caro Baroja, *Las falsificaciones de la historia* (Barcelona, 1992), 49-158.

something, as in the case of the papal claim to the States of the Church, or to prove something, such as the harmony of paganism and Christianity, or (in the case of Annius), the Egyptian origins of civilisation and the antiquity of the history of Spain, or (in the case of the lead books) the long tradition of Christianity among speakers of Arabic in Andalusia.

Exposures of forged documents were an off-shoot of the process of 'textual criticism', the attempt by humanists to reconstruct texts as their original authors (usually ancient Greeks or Romans) had written them, texts which had been corrupted by copyists over the centuries. In the course of 'emending' texts in this way, it was obviously necessary to consider whether or not a given text had been correctly attributed to its author. The critique of the Donation of Constantine by the Roman humanist Lorenzo Valla, who showed conclusively that the text had been written centuries later than it purported, is simply the most famous of a series of such demonstrations by leading humanists from Petrarch onwards.[3]

The *Outline of Scepticism* by the ancient philosopher Sextus Empiricus, which argues against the possibility of knowing the past, was rediscovered by the humanists in the course of their hunt for classical texts.[4] At much the same time, general discussions of the problem of historical knowledge are recorded for the first time since classical antiquity. Heinrich Cornelius Agrippa, for instance, wrote a book entitled the *Vanity of the Sciences*, in the course of which he dismissed history as untrustworthy. Agrippa's argument was repeated by the Spanish humanist Juan Luis Vives and discussed by the Italian critic Francesco Robortello.[5] Again, in one of his *Ten Dialogues on History* (1560) the Italian philosopher Francesco Patrizzi included a discussion of 'the truth of history', focussing on the problem of contradictory accounts of the same

---

[3] Franco Gaeta, *Lorenzo Valla: filologia e storia nell'umanesimo italiano* (Naples, 1955); Donald Kelley, *Foundations of Modern Historical Scholarship* (New York, 1970), 19-52.
[4] Richard Popkin, *The History of Scepticism from Savonarola to Bayle* (1960: 3rd edn, Oxford 2003), 17-43.
[5] Julian H. Franklin, *Jean Bodin and the sixteenth-century revolution in the methodology of law and history* (New York, 1963), 89-102.

event. Today, the best-known of these Renaissance discussions is surely Sir Philip Sidney's *Defence of Poetry* against its critics, in which the author launched a pre-emptive strike on history, mocking the historian as someone 'loden with old mouse-eaten records', yet 'for the most part authorising himself on the notable foundations of hearsay'.

These discussions of the unreliability of history are brief and many of them lack concrete examples, giving the impression that they are rhetorical exercises rather than expressions of genuine concern. More can be learned about Renaissance attitudes from debates focussed on specific texts. For example, the famous historian of the Indies, Fernando Gonzales de Oviedo, distinguishing 'true history' from 'fables' and criticized his rival Pietro Martire of Anghiera for offering unreliable knowledge derived from books, contrasting this with his own eyewitness accounts. In similar fashion, the soldier Bernal Diáz called his own account of the conquest of Mexico a *historia verdadera* in order to contrast it with a rival history by Lopez de Gómara.

At much the same time as Oviedo the Spanish Franciscan preacher and moralist Antonio de Guevara wrote a biography of the Roman emperor Marcus Aurelius, who was a kind of philosopher-king. As its title *The Dial of Princes* (1529) makes clear, the biography was intended to offer a good example to rulers in the manner of the lives of the saints or Xenophon's *Cyropaedia*, which was much read at this time (there were at least twelve editions in the sixteenth century, in Greek, Latin, Italian French and English). However, Guevara was criticized by a certain Pedro de Rua for having invented certain historical details in his biography of Marcus Aurelius.

What makes the Rua-Guevara debate particularly significant is the fact that Guevara defended himself by claiming that reading history was little more than a pastime, since in the case of the Trojan War, for example, little or nothing could be safely asserted. He concluded that so far as secular and pagan histories are concerned 'we have no certainty that some tell the truth more than others', because there are arguments on both sides. Rua's reaction to Guevara's conclusion, or more exactly to his refusal to reach a conclusion, was to compare his adversary with Pyrrho of Elis and other 'sceptical philosophers'. Whether or not Guevara's letter is authentic (and even this matter is disputed), fray Antonio was indeed sympathetic to scepticism and liked to quote the remark attributed to the ancient Roman Pliny that 'Nothing is more certain in this life than that everything is uncertain'.[6]

In his classic study of the history of modern scepticism, Richard Popkin argued that sceptical attitudes were encouraged by the Reformation, since both Catholics and Protestants proved more skilful at undermining each other's arguments than at supporting their own. Protestants subverted the traditional trust in tradition, while Catholics undermined the authority of Scripture. The sceptical Calvinist Pierre Bayle made a similar point, describing both tradition and the Bible as 'noses of wax' that could be twisted in different directions, 'good arguments for historical pyrrhonism'.[7] This argument may be given a historiographical twist, focussing on Catholic and Protestant historians of the Church, notably the Protestant team known as the 'Centuriators of Magdeburg' on one side and Cardinal Baronio on the other.[8] For example, Valla's exposure of the Donation of Constantine was printed for the first time by the German reformer Ulrich Hutten, and employed by the Centuriators in their attack on the Pope. On the other hand, the Centuriators and other Protestants accepted the story of a female pope, Papesse Jeanne or 'Pope Joan', a story that was rejected as mere 'fable' by the Catholics.[9]

More generally, the debate over the Reformation encouraged awareness of the problem of partiality or bias in historical writing. Two historians, the German humanist Johannes Sleidanus in his *Commentaries* (1545) and the Frenchman Henri La Popelinière, in

---

[6] William Nelson, *Fact or Fiction: the dilemma of the Renaissance storyteller* (Cambridge MA, 1973), 35-6.
[7] Popkin, *Scepticism*, 3-17. Bayle quoted in Hubert Bost, 'Histoire et critique d'histoire chez Pierre Bayle', *Revue d'histoire et de philosophie religieuses* 70 (1990), 69-108, at 99.
[8] Heinz Scheible, *Die Entstehung der Magdeburger Zenturien* (Gütersloh, 1966); Stefano Zen, *Baronio storico: controriforma e crisi del metodo umanistico* (Naples, 1994).
[9] Bietenholz, *Historia*, 97-107; Alain Boureau, *The Myth of Pope Joan* (1988: English translation, Chicago IL, 2001).

The True History of the Late Troubles (1571) presented themselves as impartial narrators, concerned only, in the phrase that Ranke would later make famous, with 'what actually happened': in the words of Sleidanus, *prout res quoque acta fuit*, or as La Popelinière put it, *réciter la chose comme elle est advenue*. The problem of bias would attract still more attention in the seventeenth century, as we shall see.

The seventeenth-century crisis

In a famous study, Paul Hazard vividly described what he called the European 'crisis of consciousness' of the late seventeenth century.[10] It included what might be called a 'crisis of historical consciousness', in the sense of increasingly frequent and radical criticisms of traditional historical practice.

For example, this period witnessed a reaction against the use of rhetoric in works of history. Giambattista Birago Avogadro, in his *History of the Revolutions of the Kingdom of Portugal* (1646) which was concerned with the recent rebellion against Spanish rule, admitted that his book was open to criticism as lacking in eloquence, but claimed that his account was faithful to the truth and supported by the documents.

There was also a reaction against invented speeches, so often put into the mouths of political and military leaders by their historians in the fifteenth and sixteenth centuries. In the preface to his *Annals* (1615-27) concerned with the reign of Queen Elizabeth, William Camden declared that he had 'thrust in no orations but such as were truly spoken; or those reduced to fewer words; much less have I feigned any'. In similar fashion he deliberately avoided digressions and *sententiae*, both important elements in the tradition. He was aware of the potential clash between history and poetry.

Again, in deliberate contrast with the practice of most classical and Renaissance historians, the Venetian friar Paolo Sarpi excluded orations from his *History of the Council of Trent* (1619).

[10] Paul Hazard, *Crise de la conscience européenne* (1935: English translation, *The European mind (1680-1715)* (London, 1953).

His decision was all the more remarkable because speech-making was one of the major activities of the Council. Sarpi summarized these discourses in indirect speech, rather than attempting to reproduce the words spoken at the time.[11]

More radical than the reaction against rhetoric was the critique of historical knowledge formulated in the course of the epistemological debates of the seventeenth century. Three French philosophers in particular played an important part in the articulation of this debate: René Descartes, François La Mothe Le Vayer and Pierre Bayle. The discussion of historical scepticism or 'pyrrhonism' became an international one and continued well into the eighteenth century.[12]

The problem was the failure of historical knowledge to measure up to strict standards of certainty, notably the epistemological standards formulated by René Descartes. In his search for firm foundations for knowledge in his *Discourse on Method* (1637), Descartes dismissed written history and fiction (*les histoires and les fables*, as he called them) on similar grounds. The problem with fables is that they 'make one imagine events as possible that are not'. As for history,

Even the most reliable histories, even if they do not change or augment the value of what happened, to make it more worthy of being read, at least they almost always omit the lowest and least illustrious circumstances. As a result, what is left does not appear as it is, so that those people who model their conduct on the examples that they take from it are liable to fall into the exaggerations of the paladins of our romances, and to make plans that they are not capable of carrying out.

In other words, Descartes rested his case for the futility of studying history on the harm done by following the traditional

---

[11] Peter Burke, 'The Rhetoric and Anti-Rhetoric of History in the Early Seventeenth Century', in *Anamorphosen der Rhetorik: Die Wahrheitspiel der Renaissance*, ed. Gerhard Schröder et al. (Munich, 1997), 71-9.

[12] Carlo Borghero, *La certezza e la storia: cartesianismo, pirronismo e conoscenza storica* (Milan, 1983); Markus Völkel, *'"Pyrrhonismus historicus" und "fides historica": Die Entwicklung der deutschen historischen Methodologie unter dem Gesichtspunkt der historischen Skepsis* (Frankfurt, 1987). Cf. Martin Mulsow, 'Cartesianismus, Pyrrhonismus and historische Kritik', *Philosophische Rundschau* 42 (1995), 297-314.

principle of the 'dignity of history'. The reference to the 'paladins' echoes the mockery of romances of chivalry by Cervantes, and may even be intended as an allusion to *Don Quixote*. Descartes thus focussed attention on the relation between content and form, raising the crucial problem of the criteria according to which historians select or omit information. A critique of historical knowledge was also offered by Descartes' contemporary Gassendi and his follower Malebranche. However, the undermining of what, following Descartes' architectural metaphor, he called the 'great building of history' was carried still further by La Mothe Le Vayer and also by Bayle.

François La Mothe Le Vayer, a member of the group of so-called *libertins érudits* in Paris, admirers of Montaigne, wrote a *Discourse on History* (1638, a year after the *Discourse on Method*) later amplified and re-titled *The Uncertainty of History* (1668). La Mothe was close to Descartes in his criticism of the conventions of the high style which require the omission of whatever cannot be discussed in an elegant manner, and he also noted contradictions between different accounts of the same event, such as the battle of Pavia.[13]

As for Pierre Bayle, a Protestant pastor in exile in Rotterdam, scepticism was central to his famous *Historical and Critical Dictionary* (1695-7), a work of reference which might be better described as a contribution to ignorance than as a contribution to knowledge, since Bayle's main aim was to show the unreliability of received accounts of the past, such as the ones in the historical dictionary compiled by his predecessor Louis Moreri.[14]

By the early eighteenth century, the debate on historical knowledge had come to involve scholars and thinkers outside France. In the Netherlands, for instance, they included Jacob Perizonius; In England, Lord Bolingbroke; in Italy, Ludovico Muratori; in Spain, Benito Feyjóo; while in Germany, where the

---

[13] Popkin, *Scepticism*, 80-7; Borghero, *La certezza*; V. I. Comparato, 'La Mothe dalla critica storica al pirronismo', in Tullio Gregory, ed., *Ricerche su letteratura libertina e letteratura clandestina nel seicento* (Florence, 1981), 259-80.

[14] Ruth Whelan, *Anatomy of superstition: a study of the historical theory and practice of Pierre Bayle* (Oxford, 1989).

study of history had a relatively important place in the university curriculum, there were almost fifty academic contributions.[15]

The same basic arguments were put forward again and again, so that it is better to summarize the debate theme by theme, rather than individual by individual. Following the traditional analogy between history and law, we might describe the arguments used by the critics as the case for the prosecution, imagining Clio in the dock. The prosecution rested its case on two principal arguments. The first was the argument from bias, the second the argument from forgery.

The problem of bias

In their own time, ancient historians (notably Herodotus) were sometimes criticized for distorting the truth, and these criticisms had been revived at the Renaissance. Modern historians were attacked for the same reasons. The general problem these criticisms illustrate is the problem of partiality or bias. Montaigne's essay 'On books' (1580) criticizes historians who like to draw a moral lesson from the past and cannot avoid 'distorting and twisting the story according to this bias' [*contourner et tordre la narration à ce biais*].[16]

'Bias' is a metaphor derived from the game of bowls, to which the dons of Oxford and Cambridge were particularly addicted in the seventeenth century. Perhaps this is how the term came to be applied to deviations from the true path in politics and religion. The accusation of bias might refer to conscious manipulation, but the term was also used to suggest that our passions and our interests prevent us from seeing beyond our own side – whether this was a church, a nation or a political 'party' – a term that was beginning to come into use in the seventeenth century, as in the English case of Whigs versus Tories.

---

[15] Borghero, *La certezza*; on Germany, Markus Völkel, 'Pyrrhonismus historicus' *und* 'fides historica': *Die Entwicklung der deutschen historischen Methodologie unter dem Gesichtspunkt der historischen Skepsis* (Frankfurt, 1987).
[16] Michel de Montaigne, *Essays*, Book 2, ch. 10.

In similar fashion to Montaigne, the scholar Gabriel Naudé, an admirer of his, noted that historians, 'with the exception of those who are quite heroic', never represent things as they are [*ne nous representent jamais les choses pures*], but 'slant and mask them according to the image they wish to project [*les inclinent et masquent selon le visage qu'ils leur veulent prendre*]. La Mothe also had much to say about the problem of bias. What would our image of the Punic wars be today, he asked rhetorically, if we had access to an account from the Carthaginian point of view as well as that of the Romans? How would Caesar's Gallic wars now appear if Vercingetorix rather than Caesar had been the one to write his *Commentaries*?

As so often happened in this period, concern with modern examples underlay the quotation of ancient ones, and La Mothe, who worked for Cardinal Richelieu, was especially concerned with the bias of Spanish historians in their accounts of wars with France. He criticized the Spanish historian Prudencio de Sandoval (c1560-1621), official historian to Philip III of Spain, for 'calumny' and 'partiality', including his consistent attribution of valour to the Spanish troops alone in their conflicts with the French. Widening his criticisms, La Mothe pointed out that other Spanish historians also diminished French valour, and that in earlier periods biographers such as Eusebius and Eginhard had flattered the emperors about whom they wrote, Constantine and Charlemagne.

One of the readers delighted by La Mothe's attack on Sandoval and others was the sceptical philosopher Pierre Bayle: 'How I love to see someone mock the bias of historians', he wrote. 'There is no greater deception (*filouterie*) greater than that which can be exercised on historical monuments'. 'I hardly ever read historians with the intention of discovering what has happened', Bayle confessed, 'but only to learn what is said in each nation and in each party'. What Bayle found most interesting in a work of history was precisely the prejudice it revealed. In the case of the French Wars of Religion, viewed so differently by Catholics and by Protestants, he said he believed little more than that the

Protestants were sometimes armed and that battles took place at Jarnac and Moncontour.

The French were not alone in their preoccupation with bias. In England, for instance, Edmund Bolton claimed that although in theory 'Indifferency and even dealing are the Glory of historians', in practice 'all late authors that ever yet I could read among us, convey with them to Narrations of things done fifteen or sixteen hundred years past the Jealousies Passions and Affections of their own Time'.

In Germany, Gottfried Wilhelm Leibniz, who like Bayle combined interests in philosophy and history, was interested in the problem of bias and distinguished three kinds; 'from venality' as in the case of Giovio; 'from ambition', as in the case of the French historian Scipion Dupleix, and the bias to be found in the sources themselves. Again, in a study with the unforgettable title, *On the Charlatanry of the Learned* (1717), the German scholar J. B. Mencken, an acquaintance of Bayle's, emphasised the diversity of judgements on the leading figures of antiquity by the classical historians themselves. 'Ammianus Marcellinus and Montanus commend Julian [Roman emperor, nicknamed 'the Apostate'] as a paragon of virtue; others censure him as a monster of vice. Dio condemns the deeds of Brutus and Cassius; Plutarch extols them. To Paterculus, Sejanus is a lovable man; to many others, he is odious.'

The majority of examples cited so far have been political, but the problem of bias was often discussed in a religious context. As we have seen, the ideal of narrating 'what actually happened' was put forward in the context of the religious wars. Bayle's remarks on bias were occasioned by the publication of an anti-Calvinist history of Calvinism by an ex-Jesuit, Louis Maimbourg that was published shortly before Louis XIV decided to expel Protestants from his kingdom.[17] For their part, Catholics drew attention to the bias of Sarpi's notoriously anti-papal *History of the Council of Trent* published in 1619. The German Protestant Gottfried Arnold offended almost everyone by what he called his

---

[17] Bost, 'Histoire et critique'.

'unpartisan' (*unparteische*) history of Christianity (1699) which attempted to be fair to the orthodox and heretics alike. The debate continued into the eighteenth century, when the German scholar Johann Friedrich Burscher produced a formula close to Ranke's when he declared that the historian 'must present a fact just as it happened' (*Er muss die Sache so vorstellen, wir sie Geschehen ist*).[18]

Thus Voltaire was not saying anything radically new but rather summing up more than a century of debate when he wrote his essay *Historical Pyrrhonism* (1769), which like La Mothe discussed the bias of Roman historians against Carthage. 'In order to judge fairly it would be necessary to have access to the archives of Hannibal's family'. Since he was Voltaire, he could not resist expressing the wish that he could also see the memoirs of Caiphas and Pontius Pilate. He also noted the political bias of historians attached to parties such as the Whigs and Tories.

The problem of bias is a universal one, but it was also a topical problem in the seventeenth century, for two reasons; the rise of religious wars and the formation of the centralized state. The religious wars of 1568-1648 were fought with ink and paper as well as with guns and swords, and contrasting interpretations of history were crucial in these polemics. Each 'party', whether religious or political, tried to present its own version of recent events and to 'unmask' the misrepresentations in the enemy version.

The case of the 'Anhalt Chancery' illustrates the process in an extremely concrete way. After the defeat of the Calvinist prince Frederick V by imperial forces at the battle of the White Mountain in 1621, the papers of his follower Christian of Anhalt fell into the hands of the imperialists. They instantly produced a pamphlet, called *The Anhalt Chancery*, in order to pin the 'war-guilt' on to their enemies. The following year, one of the generals on the other side, Ernst von Mansfeld, captured an imperial courier, and a rival and opposing pamphlet called *The Spanish Chancery* duly appeared, blaming the Habsburgs for the war.[19] Whether

---

[18] Quoted in L. E. Kurth (1964) 'Historiographie und historischer Roman: Kritik und Theorie im 18. Jht', *Modern Language Notes* 79 (1964), 337-64, at 340.

[19] R. Koser, *Der Kanzleienstreit* (Halle, 1874).

the couriers and their documents really existed or not, the rise of this technique of persuasion deserves to be noted.

These circumstances encouraged the rise of what may be called 'official history'. Official historians were not uncommon in the Renaissance, working for the republics of Florence and Venice and also for new dynasties from Portugal to Hungary. However, their numbers multiplied in the seventeenth century. Assemblies, such as the Dutch States-General, and religious orders, such as the Jesuits, commissioned accounts of their activities. So, above all, did monarchs. Queen Elizabeth commissioned William Camden. Louis XIII commissioned Scipion Dupleix to present him as 'Louis the Just'. Louis XIV commissioned Boileau and Racine (among others) to show him as 'Louis the Great'. The emperor Leopold commissioned Galeazzo Gualdo Priorato and Charles II commissioned John Dryden, while the rulers of Prussia and Sweden both commissioned Samuel Pufendorf. Awareness of these commissions and of the pressures on official historians to show their masters in a glorious light is likely to have encouraged scepticism about the reliability of earlier accounts of past events.

The problem of authenticity

The second major argument for the prosecution was even more fundamental than the argument from bias. Historians were charged with credulity. They were accused of basing their accounts of the past on forged documents and of writing about characters who never existed and events which never took place.

As we have seen, the humanists of the Renaissance had already exposed a number of forged documents, as well as producing some more. New texts of this kind were produced in the seventeenth century, especially in Spain, including the chronicle of the monk 'Haubertus', published in 1667.[20]

However, the seventeenth-century critiques were more serious than earlier ones in the sense of challenging the credibility of

---

[20] Caro Baroja, *Falsificaciones*, 97-102.

more and more texts, including some of the most fundamental texts in both the classical and Christian traditions. Indeed, the term 'critic' – which is etymologically related to 'crisis' – came into use at this time partly to refer to these exposures.[21]

It was at this time that the so-called 'hermetic' writings attributed to the Egyptian sage Hermes Trismegistus were re-dated by the French Protestant scholar Isaac Casaubon. [22] Dares and Dictys, the supposed historians of the Trojan War, were now dismissed as forgeries. So were the letters of the Greek ruler Phalaris, exposed by the great classical scholar Richard Bentley in his famous *Dissertation on the Epistles of Phalaris* (1697).[23] So was the history of Carthage attributed to Sanchoniathon, and even the records of the magistrates and pontiffs of ancient Rome.

Among the most powerful arguments employed by the critics was the argument from 'anachronism', a new word in the seventeenth century. The anachronisms exposed ranged from the language of the forged documents to references to people or events about which the supposed authors could not have known. Casaubon, for instance, pointed out that the hermetic writings referred to the sculptor Phidias, who lived centuries after the texts were supposed to have been written.

On the same criteria, the Bible was approached in a critical manner. Baruch Spinoza and Thomas Hobbes both challenged the attribution of the Pentateuch to Moses on the grounds that the death of Moses is recounted in the text. Some texts attributed to the Fathers of the Church were also called into doubt, notably by the Calvinist scholar Jean Daillé. So were some medieval documents, including papal decretals, Icelandic sagas and charters issued by the Merovingian kings.

A French Jesuit named Jean Hardouin went so far as to claim that the majority of classical texts were forgeries. It was in 1693 that he began, he wrote, 'to scent fraud' in texts attributed to St Augustine, a fraud perpetrated 'about four hundred years ago' by what he called 'the criminal faction' (*scelerata grex*), who anticipated

---
[21] Jean Jehasse, *La Renaissance de la critique* (1976: second edition, Paris 2002).
[22] Grafton, *Defenders*, 145-61.
[23] Joseph Levine, *Ancients and Moderns*, (Ithaca NY, 1991)

the Calvinists and Jansenists. The monasteries of Corbey, Fleury and Bobbio were centres of this 'conspiracy', while the great period of forgery extended from the fourteenth to the sixteenth century. The conspirators forged not only the Fathers but Cicero and Virgil, 'imaginary adversaries', decrees, canons and charters'. Hence ecclesiastical history from 500 onwards, like ancient Greek and Roman history, was dismissed as fabulous. As in the case of the Reformation debates, seventeenth-century religious controversies such as the battle between Jesuits and Jansenists, encouraged scepticism. The Jansenists, who believed that only a minority of Chrsitians would be saved, appealed for support to the writings of St Augustine, while Hardouin 'began to scent fraud', as he put it, in 'Augustine and his contemporaries', before he extended his scepticism backwards to include classical texts. Hardouin has been called 'pathological' and would now be diagnosed as paranoid – after all, he believed in a `conspiracy' to forge texts. However, he was only an extreme example of a general trend, combining the doubts already expressed about many of these documents as well as adding a few of his own.[24]

The crisis

The example of Hardouin shows how these specific challenges might have a cumulative effect. No wonder that in 1700 an Italian scholar, Gianvicenzo Gravina, described his own time as the 'age of criticism', or that the word 'critical' became a fashionable one for book titles, especially in France: the *Histoire Critique du Vieux Testament* (1678) by the Oratorian priest Richard Simon, for instance, Bayle's *Dictionnaire Historique et Critique*, or the *Histoire Critique des Pratiques Superstitieuses* (1702) by another Oratorian, Pierre Lebrun.

An increasing amount of what had been accepted as true history

---

[24] Jean Sgard, 'Et si les anciens étaient modernes. ... le système du P. Hardouin', in Louise Godard de Donville (ed.) *D'un siècle à l'autre* (Marseille, 1987), 209-20; Anthony Grafton, 'Jean Hardouin: the Antiquary as Pariah', *Journal of the Warburg and Courtauld Institutes* 62 (1999), 241-67.

– the foundation of ancient Rome by Romulus, for example, the lives of certain saints, or the foundation of the French monarchy by Pharamond, was now being dismissed as invention. Did Pharamond exist? scholars asked. Did Romulus exist? Did Aeneas ever go to Italy? Did the Trojan War take place, or was it just the subject of Homer's 'romance'? The debate on early Roman history was particularly vigorous in the early eighteenth century, the main forum being the French Academy of Inscriptions, where a paper 'on the uncertainty of the first four centuries of Roman history' stirred up a major controversy.[25]

Stories about national origins came under particularly heavy fire. La Mothe noted the absurdity of Sandoval's genealogy of Habsburgs, which went back to Adam. The Protestant scholar Samuel Bochart remarked on the 'folly' of tracing the French and other modern peoples back to Troy, while the Jesuit Gabriel Daniel agreed that Trojan origins were 'pure fable'.. Giambattista Vico generalized from examples such as these when he formulated his famous axiom in the *New Science* about the 'conceit of nations' (*boria delle nazioni*); 'Every nation ... has the same conceit that it before all other nations invented the comforts of human life'.

Following in the footsteps of Descartes and his systematic doubt, some scholars went still further, at least in their thought-experiments. Did Charles V exist? Did Augustus exist? Did the siege of La Rochelle really take place?

Responses to crisis

Historians had either to find an answer to sceptics or go out of business. They did find an answer, or to be more exact, they found a number of different answers which between them permitted what has been called the 'rehabilitation' of history or as contemporaries put it, 'the trustworthiness of historians' (*fides historica*).[26]

---

[25] Mouza Raskolnikoff, *Histoire romaine et critique historique dans l'Europe des Lumières* (Paris, 1992).
[26] Judith Shklar, 'Jean D'Alembert and the Rehabilitation of History', *Journal of the History of Ideas* 42 (1981), 643-64.

One of the apparent exits from the crisis turned out to be a blind alley, and to be perceived as such by some scholars of the period. This was the geometrical method, so prestigious in the late seventeenth century. Pierre-Daniel Huet, for instance, tried to establish the truth of Christianity as a historical religion on the basis of 'axioms' such as the following: 'Every historical work is truthful, if it tells what happened in the way in which the events are told in many books which are contemporary or more or less contemporary to the events narrated'.[27]

Again, a Scottish theologian, John Craig, formulated his *Rules of Historical Evidence* (1699) in the form of axioms and theorems. Unfortunately these axioms and theorems turn out to be rather banal, using the language of mathematics and physics to restate commonplaces, for example the principle that the reliability of sources varies with the distance of the source from the event recorded.[28] As Nicolas Fréret pointed out early in the eighteenth century, Craig was pursuing the illusion of a perfect certainty which cannot be found in morals, politics or history.

Sources

More productive and more useful than the geometrical method was the emphasis on original documents. Reviewing Rymer's *Foedera*, a collection of the original text of treaties, the critic Jean Leclerc made the point that compilations of this kind were a means of refuting pyrrhonism.

The critique of documents had a positive side as well as a negative one. Responding to the Jesuit Papebroch, who had questioned the authenticity of royal charters in early medieval France, the great Benedictine scholar Jean Mabillon produced a treatise, *On Diplomatic* (1681), discussing the methods of dating such documents by the study of their handwriting,

---

[27] April G. Shelford, 'Thinking geometrically in Pierre-Daniel Huet's *Demonstratio Evangelica*', *Journal of the History of Ideas* 63 (2000), 599-618.

[28] Lorraine Daston, *Classical Probability in the Enlightenment* (Princeton NJ, 1988), 313-16, 333-4.

their formulae, their seals and so on, showing in this way how forgeries might be detected and the authenticity of other charters vindicated. This was not the first work to discuss medieval charters in this way, but it was by far the most systematic. Mabillon convinced his opponent, as the latter was generous enough to admit.[29] There was no single definitive reply to Hardouin as there was to Papebroch, and perhaps there was no need for one. However, Jean Le Clerc did produce a useful handbook, the *Art of Criticism* (1697) which laid out the rules of textual criticism, classical and biblical.

The techniques elaborated by Mabillon and others have become known as 'source criticism'. Renaissance humanists such as Erasmus frequently spoke of the need to return 'to the sources' [*ad fontes*], while he English scholar John Selden used to refer to the 'fountains'. A similar idea was that of 'originals', as in the proud phrase of Bernard de Montfaucon in the preface to his history of the French monarchy. 'I have composed this history on the basis of the originals themselves' [*j'ai composé cette histoire sur les originaux mêmes*]

In the course of the seventeenth and eighteenth centuries, the language of historians came to include more and more references to 'proofs', 'pièces justificatives', 'pièces authentiques', 'monuments' (in the sense of ancient texts), 'evidence', and 'testimony'. The legal language of 'eyewitnesses' and 'testimony' is worth noting. Thomas Sherlock's *The Trial of the Witnesses of the Resurrection of Jesus* (1729) was presented as if in a court of law, while the Jesuit Henri Griffet made an elaborate comparison between the task of a historian and that of a judge. Linked to the increasing awareness of the need for evidence was the rise of the reference, whether footnote, endnote or marginal note.[30]

Witnesses needed to be cross-examined and some scholars, such as Jacobus Perizonius, in his *Truth of Histories* (1702), offered rules for the detection of bias, suggesting that the trustworthiness of a text depended on the age, nationality, education and

---

[29] M. David Knowles, 'Jean Mabillon, *Journal of Ecclesiastical History* 10 (1959), 153-73; Blandine Barret-Kriegel, *La défaite de l'érudition* (Paris, 1988).
[30] Anthony Grafton, *A Short History of the Footnote* (Cambridge MA, 1997).

character of its author and distinguishing unreliable writers like Maimbourg and Varillas from trustworthy historians such as Thucydides and Commynes.

Another response to the sceptics was to emphasize the relative reliability of the evidence from material culture, notably inscriptions, coins and medals. Montfaucon, for instance, edited ten volumes of images which represented and explained ancient history: *Antiquité expliquée et représentée en figures*. When he reached the eleventh century, Montfaucon discussed and illustrated the Bayeux Tapestry. In the field of material culture, the notorious father Hardouin was not a sceptic but an enthusiast, who believed that the only way of establishing a satisfactory chronology of ancient history was to rely on the testimony of coins rather than on the assertions of ancient writers. Inscriptions, coins and medals could of course be forged, but as in the case of texts, rules for the detection of such forgeries could be worked out, and the Italian scholar Scipione Maffei wrote *The Art of Lapidary Criticism* (1765).

Thus the debate with the sceptics had the unintended consequence of encouraging historians to make increasing use of non-literary sources not only for ancient history but for that of the Middle Ages as well.[31]

The Rehabilitation of Myth

Yet another response to the challenge of pyrrhonism was what has been called the 'rehabilitation of myth'. The meaning of myths, generally known in this period as 'fables' was discussed with renewed interest and often in a comparative framework. For example, in his *Origin of Fables* (1724), Bernard de Fontenelle described Greek mythology (which he compared with the Chinese and the 'American', in other words the myths of the Incas) as a mass of falsehoods, but he also noted that fables were both the history and the philosophy of those 'rude ages' (*siècles grossiers*). Similar views, expressed in more detail and with more

[31] Francis Haskell, *History and its images: art and the interpretation of the past* (New Haven CN, 1993).

sympathy for early times, were put forward by Giambattista Vico and Christian Gottlob Heyne.

Vico was a sceptic in the sense that he considered all accounts of the origins of nations to be uncertain, apart from that of the Jews. In the case of Rome, for example, it was impossible to know what happened before the second Punic War. On the other hand, Vico was an anti-sceptic or a 'critic of criticism' in the sense that he believed that myths were originally 'true stories' in the sense that they expressed 'the mode of thought of whole peoples'. As Bayle had read historians as evidence of prejudice, so Vico read myth as evidence of changing viewpoints or mentalities. In similar fashion Heyne, a professor of classics at Göttingen, presented what he called 'fables' or 'mythical discourse' (*sermo mythicus*) as both true and rational, the philosophy and the history of the childhood of humanity.[32] This view, still unorthodox in the late eighteenth century, would become the new conventional wisdom after 1800, especially in the circles of German Romantics such as Friedrich Schlegel and Friedrich Schelling.

Towards a Resolution

Drawing on the more limited studies already mentioned, a number of general refutations of historical pyrrhonism appeared in the late seventeenth and early eighteenth centuries.[33] The key argument against the sceptics was the one about 'degrees of assent' put forward by John Locke in his *Essay Concerning Human Understanding* (1690): 'When any particular matter of fact is vouched by concurrent testimony of unsuspected witnesses, there our consent is ... unavoidable'. For example, 'that there is such a city in Italy as Rome; that about 1700 years ago there lived in it a man, called Julius Caesar; that he was a general, and that he won a battle against another, called Pompey'.

---

[32] On Vico, Joseph Mali, *The Rehabilitation of Myth* (Cambridge, 1992); on Heyne, Luigi Marini, *I maestri della Germania: Göttingen 1770-1820* (Turin, 1975), 254-70, and Bietenholz, *Historia*, 256-8, 284-8.

[33] Borghero, *La certezza*.

Like Locke, Gerhard Patje (or his academic supervisor, Friedrich Bierling), in his dissertation *Historical Pyrrhonism* (1707) distinguished levels of certainty or probability in history, three in all, from the maximum (that Julius Caesar existed) via the middle level (the reasons for the abdication of Charles V) to the minimum (the problem of the complicity of Mary Queen of Scots in the murder of her husband, or of Wallenstein's plans in the months before his assassination). The use of modern examples in place of the staple ancient ones is worth noting.

Again, Fréret's critique of what he called 'the historical pyrrhonism which is so fashionable in our time' depended on the distinction not only between truth and falsehood but also 'between different degrees of probability'. His rehabilitation of history included not only a defence of written testimonies, but also arguments in favour of 'unwritten tradition' [*la tradition non écrite*] Fréret was well aware of oral tradition's propensity to change and he granted it a lesser degree of reliability than texts, but he defended it all the same. We must not imagine that the rediscovery of oral tradition by historians is altogether the achievement of our own time.

By the middle of the eighteenth century, at the latest, one may say that the crisis of historical consciousness was considered to be resolved. Voltaire's contribution to the debate, however entertaining, came rather too late to be useful. From the scholar's point of view, the merit of the sceptics had been to provoke scholars to distinguish different degrees of probability, to formulate practical rules for the criticism of different types of source, and to be more suspicious of 'empty conjectures' about hidden motives, in the style of the secret histories.

Secret histories, gazettes and novels

The crisis of pyrrhonism also had consequences beyond the domain of historical scholarship. It is scarcely surprising to find that the relation between history and fiction, already discussed in the Renaissance, as we have seen, was examined with particular interest during the crisis. For some scholars, the distinction between history and fiction was clear and distinct, so that describing a colleague as a writer of 'romances' was a way of rejecting his work. Leibniz expressed his contempt for the legend that Britain had been founded by Brutus the Trojan by comparing the story to the once-famous romance *Amadis de Gaule*. The historian of the Reformation Gilbert Burnet condemned the French historian Varillas because 'his books had too much the air of a romance', only to be denounced in his turn for exactly the same failing. In 1710, a man from Padua was denounced to the Inquisition for calling the Bible a 'holy novel' [*sacro romanzo*].[34]

Examples of this kind of criticism could be multiplied, but it may be more interesting to note the existence of the less conventional view that historians had something to learn from novelists. Thus Louis Maimbourg, whose history of Calvinism provoked Bayle's critique, tried to ensure that his way of writing history would give his readers 'the pleasure of a romance'. Even Leibniz wished for 'a little of a romance' (*un peu de roman*) in historical writings, especially when motives were being discussed.

The authors of the so-called 'secret histories', a new genre which proliferated in the late seventeenth century, certainly gave Leibniz what he wanted. The name 'secret history' was borrowed from the sixth-century Byzantine historian Procopius, whose scandalous account of the doings of the empress Theodora had been published in 1623. Like the modern gossip column, these histories made use of the idiom of intimacy. Their claim to authority was based on their supposed ability to go behind the scenes of public life.[35]

Among the most famous French secret histories were two studies of Florence under the Medici, Varillas' *Anecdotes of Florence, or Secret History of the House of Medici* (1685) and Lenoble's *Secret History of the Pazzi Conspiracy* (1697). In England,

[34] Q. Barbierato 2006, 167.
[35] Peter Burke, 'Publicizing the Private: the rise of "secret history"', in Christian Emden and David Midgley, eds., *Changing Perceptions of the Public Sphere* (Oxford, 2012), 57-72.

secret history dared to be more topical, as in the case of Mrs Manley's *The Secret History of Queen Zarah* (1705), about the role of Queen Anne's favourite, Sarah Churchill, and a series of publications by Daniel Defoe, including *The Secret History of the October Club* (1711).

Secret history was among other things a response to the weaknesses of humanist history, written in the high style and emphasizing high motives and the effectiveness of political and military leaders. These weaknesses were pitilessly exposed by Descartes, as we have seen. The secret historians, on the other hand, claimed that great events had petty causes, a claim discussed at a general level in an essay by the novelist Saint-Réal and brilliantly summarized in Pascal's epigram 'Cleopatra's nose, had it been shorter, the whole face of the world would have been changed'. Secret history may also be regarded as an antidote to 'official history', which was becoming increasingly important, as we have seen. It was obvious that official historians were not telling the whole truth. Authors and publishers alike realized that there was a market for alternative stories, unofficial versions of the past, whether they were presented as histories or romances.

The unofficial or secret historians were sometimes described with more or less contempt as mere journalists or as novelists, and the relations between all three genres were close. The late seventeenth century was a time when periodicals (quarterlies, monthlies, weeklies, etc) were increasing in numbers and importance. Many of these journals were official publications but there were also unofficial journals which gave a very different account of recent events. Some 'journalists' (a term coined at this time) also wrote history in book form.

Although awareness of the discrepancy between different accounts of the same event is nothing new – think of the problem of reconciling the four gospels – this awareness was surely made more acute by the rise of journals, since divergent accounts of the same event might be published in different newspapers on the same day, or in the same paper on successive days as more information came to light.[36] One of Pierre Bayle's arguments for pyrrhonism was precisely the fact that gazettes were unreliable and that there are many 'bad historians' who produce their books simply by stitching together these 'poor pieces'.

While some historians and journalists were producing semi-fiction, writers of fiction were moving closer to history. As Huet remarked in his essay *On the Origins of Romances* (1669), in classical antiquity the difference between the genres of history and fiction was one of degree rather than kind, on one side 'truths mixed with a few falsehoods' and on the other 'falsehoods mixed with some truths'. Incidentally, Huet was a friend of both Fontenelle and the novelist Madame de Lafayette. In England, Defoe produced both fiction and secret history, while Manley's *Secret History of Queen Zara* might equally well be described as a contribution to either genre. The late seventeenth century saw the rise of the historical romance, in the sense of a story that was not only set in the past but also introduced real people and offered interpretations of historical events.

The most famous examples came from the pen of the abbé de Saint-Réal, whose *Dom Carlos*, published in 1672, bore the subtitle 'nouvelle historique', a term which soon became fashionable in France. Another well-known historical novel of the time was Boisguilbert's *Marie Stuart* (1675), telling the story of Mary Queen of Scots. In order to give readers the impression that these texts were historical sources, Saint-Réal included footnotes, while Boisguilbert claimed to be telling the 'truth', not writing a 'romance'. In the eighteenth century, they were joined by Defoe and by the abbé Prévost, who had worked briefly with Benedictine scholars before producing romances such as *Cleveland* (1731).

At a time when novel-writing was under attack from moralists, for telling lies as well as stimulating the passions, the writer Nicolas Lenglet Dufresnoy, who worked on both sides of the boundary between history and fiction, produced an apologia, *On the Use of Romances* (1734), in which he argued that

---

[36] Michael MacDonald and Terence R. Murphy, *Sleepless Souls: Suicide in Early Modern England* (Oxford, 1990), 319-20.

'the imperfection of history ought to make us esteem romances', which made no claim to be true and which gave their due place to women, who 'hardly appear in histories' despite their essential role in 'great affairs'.[37]

Pierre Bayle might well have agreed, since he enjoyed both *Dom Carlos* and other seventeenth-century historical romances. On the other hand, he disliked the 'impudence' of writers who published what claimed to be 'memoirs' (like Madame de Villedieu's Memoirs of *Henriette-Sylvie de Molière*) but were actually 'a mixture of truth and fable'.

From the late seventeenth to the late eighteenth century, invented memoirs were a fashionable literary genre in France, among them the *Mémoires de M. d'Artagnan* (which inspired *The Three Musketeers* of Alexandre Dumas), and the memoirs of the Mancini sisters, close to the young Louis XIV (the memoirs of Hortense Mancini may well have been written by Saint-Réal).[38] The fashion spread abroad, the obvious English examples being Daniel Defoe's *Memoirs of a Cavalier* and his *Journal of the Plague Year*, the latter complete with official documents and statistics to dupe the reader and give the texts what used to be called verisimilitude and what modern critics would describe as a stronger 'reality effect'. Contemporary readers appear to have taken the *Journal* to be a work of history, and it continued to be cited as a historical source in the nineteenth century.[39]

In other words, at the very time that scholars were giving more attention than every before to distinguishing fact from fiction, other writers were making successful attempts to blur the genres. Ideas and techniques such as the sense of anachronism, the use of footnotes and the practice of quoting documents supported the verisimilitude of new semi-fictional genres such as secret histories and historical romances as well as works of scholarship.

[37] Georges May, *Le dilemme du roman au 18e siècle* (New Haven and Paris, 1963), 139-61, at 141; cf. Geraldine Sheridan, *Nicolas Lenglet Dufresnoy and the Literary Underworld of the Ancien Regime* (Oxford, 1989).
[38] Vivian Mylne, *The 18th-Century French Novel* (Manchester, 1965); Marie-Thérèse Hipp, *Mythes et réalités; enquête sur le roman et les mémoires, 1660-1700* (Paris, 1976).
[39] R. Mayer, 'The Reception of the *Journal of the Plague Year* and the nexus of fiction and history in the novel', English Literary History 57 (1990), 529-56.

The interaction between written histories and works of fiction is a long-term phenomenon, running from the ancient world to our own time, and this chapter has presented only a few twists and turns in a much longer story.

Bibliography

Primary Sources

Bayle, Pierre, *Dictionnaire historique et critique* (Rotterdam, 1695-7).

Defoe, Daniel, *Journal of the Plague Year* (London, 1722).

Fontenelle, Bernard de, *De l'origine des fables* (1724: ed. J. F. Carré, Paris, 1932).

La Mothe Le Vayer, François de, *Du peu de certitude qu'il y a dans l'histoire* (Paris, 1668).

Lenglet Du Fresnoy, Nicolas, *L'histoire justifiée contre les romans* (Paris, 1735)

Saint-Réal, César de, *Dom Carlos, nouvelle historique* (1672).

Vico, Giambattista, *Scienza Nuova* (3rd edn, Naples 1744: English translation, *The New Science of Giambattista Vico*, Ithaca 1948).

Voltaire, *Pyrrhonisme de l'histoire* (1769)

Secondary Works

Bietenholz, Peter G., *Historia and Fabula: Myths and Legends in Historical Thought from Antiquity to the Modern Age* (Leiden, 1994).

Borghero, Carlo, *La certezza e la storia: cartesianesimo, pirronismo e conoscenza storica* (Milan, 1983).

Burke, Peter, 'Two Crises of Historical Consciousness', *Storia della Storiografia* no. 33 (1998), 3-16.

Davillé, Louis, *Leibniz historien* (Paris, 1909).

Grafton, Anthony, *Forgers and Critics* (Princeton, 1990).

Grafton, Anthony, *Defenders of the Text* (Princeton, 1991).

Grafton, Anthony, 'Jean Hardouin: the antiquary as pariah', *Journal of the Warburg and Courtauld Institutes* 62 (1999), 241-67.

Haskell, Francis, *History and its images: art and the interpretation of the past* (New Haven, 1993).

Hipp, Marie-Thérèse, *Mythes et réalités: enquête sur le roman et les mémoires, 1660-1700* (Paris, 1976).

Mali, Joseph, *The Rehabilitation of Myth* (Cambridge, 1992).

Momigliano, Arnaldo, *Studies in Historiography* (London, 1966).

Popkin, Richard, *History of Scepticism from Savonarola to Bayle* (1960: 3rd edn, revised and expanded, Oxford, 2003).

Chronology

1529 Guevara, *Dial of Princes*

1560 Patrizzi, *Ten Dialogues on History*

1614 Casaubon redated the *Hermetica*

1619 Sarpi, History of the Council of Trent

1637 Descartes, *Discourse on Method*

1668 La Mothe Le Vayer, *The Uncertainty of History*

1669 Huet, *Origin of Romances*

1670 Spinoza, *Theologico-Political Treatise*

1672 Saint-Réal, *Dom Carlos*

1685 Varillas, *Anecdotes of Florence*

1695-7 Bayle, *Historical and Critical Dictionary*

1697 Bentley, *Dissertation on the Epistles of Phalaris*

1697 Leclerc, *Art of Criticism*

1697 Lenoble, *Secret History of the Pazzi Conspiracy*

1699 Craig, *Rules of Historical Evidence*

1700 Courtilz, *Memoirs of d'Artagnan*

1702 Perizonius, *On the Truth of Histories*

1705 M. Manley, *The Secret History of Queen Zarah*

1707 Patje, *On Historical Pyrrhonism*

1711 Defoe, *The Secret History of the October Club*

1722 Defoe, *Journal of the Plague Year*

1724 Bierling, *On Historical Pyrrhonism*

1724 Fontenelle, *Origin of Fables*

1724 Fréret, *Reflections on the Study of Ancient Histories*

1729 Hardouin, *Critique of Ancient Writers*

1729- Montfaucon, *Monuments of the French Monarchy*

1729 Sherlock, *The Trial of the Witnesses of the Resurrection of Jesus*

1734 Lenglet, *On the Use of Novels*

1744 Vico, *New Science*, 3rd edn

1764 Heyne, *On the Causes of Fables*

1765 Maffei, *Art of Lapidary Criticism*

1769 Griffet, *Proofs of the Truth of History*

6: CO-MEMORATIONS:
PERFORMING THE PAST

This exploration starts from the cross-roads where two popular recent approaches to cultural history meet, the study of memory and the study of performance.[1] It may be useful to distinguish at the start of this essay on the performance of memory between different kinds or genres of performance. At one extreme, we find historical plays from Shakespeare to Strindberg and beyond or the historical operas of Verdi, say, or Glinka, in other words performances that are tightly organized, fully scripted and carefully rehearsed. At the other extreme, there are loosely organized, unscripted and unrehearsed attempts to re-enact past events in the sense of following past models.

In the Russian Revolution, for example, some participants, notably Trotsky, saw themselves as re-enacting the French Revolution. In 1789, some participants made comparisons between what was happening and the English Revolution of the 1640s. In 1688 in Ireland, an army officer, Captain Thomas Ash, wrote in his diary that there were rumours that the Catholics would rise and 'act over the tragedy of one thousand six hundred and forty one'.[2] In the 1640s, some Englishmen saw the events of

---
[1] Burke (2005).
[2] McBride (1997), 15-16.

the time as a kind of replay of the French religious wars of the previous century.³

In between these extremes come the regular re-enactments of historic battles such as Naseby, Gettysburg and D-Day by enthusiasts dressed in the appropriate costumes.⁴ In the middle we also find the subject of this chapter, commemorations, in other words processions, pageants, or parades (cavalcades, motorcades) that mark the anniversary and evoke the memory of a historic event.

Performances of this kind have an important role to play in the construction of what was once called 'folk memory' and is now described either as 'social' or as 'cultural' memory. Following Aleida Assmann, I shall distinguish the two terms, associating them with two traditions of scholarship, one of them German and one French. The phrase 'cultural memory' will be used to refer (as Aby Warburg did in his Mnemosyne project) to an archive or – since the theme of this chapter is performance – a repertoire of symbols, images and stereotypes which members of a given culture draw upon or re-activate whenever required, constructing what has been called a 'prosthetic memory' that is not natural in origin but, like an artificial limb, becomes part of the body.⁵

As for 'social memory', the term will be employed here to refer – following the lead of Maurice Halbwachs – to what we might call the 'cues' given to individuals by their 'memory community' (whether family, village, church, nation or all of these), in suggesting both what to remember and how to remember it. This is what some French scholars now describe as 'faire-mémoire', doubtless on the analogy of Michel de Certeau's 'faire croire'.⁶

How does the social memory work? Partly at least through participation in collective performances, as in the obvious case of 'beating the bounds' of the parish, in other words beating children so that generations later they would remember the boundaries of their community. In what follows I shall be considering a range

---

³ Salmon (1959).
⁴ Rosenzweig and Thelen (1998); Kammen (1991).
⁵ Assmann (unpublished), cf Assmann (1999); Landsberg (2004).
⁶ Davallon (1993), 9.

of performances from this point of view as 'co-memorations', in other words collaborative acts of recall or recollection.

These acts may be viewed as statements that use the language of the past to say something about the present. They are also 'performative' statements in the sense that the philosopher John Austin used the term, in other words statements that make something happen. They are rituals which 'canonize' particular events, in the sense of giving them a sacred or exemplary quality, making them 'historic' as well as historical. They reconstruct history or 're-collect' or 're-member' it in the sense of assembling fragments of the past into new patterns.

The rise of centenaries

Commemorations have a long history. As Joep Leerssen explains elsewhere in the volume in which this essay originally appeared, the jubilee, for instance, celebrated after 50 years, was a Jewish custom taken over by the early Christian Church. Centenaries by contrast were relatively rare before the seventeenth century although the ancient Egyptians celebrated one around 1200 B.C., while the emperor Antoninus Pius celebrated the 900th anniversary of the foundation of Rome.

In early modern Europe, the celebration of the Luther centenary in Northern Germany in 1617 began a trend. The event chosen for commemoration was the famous posting of the 95 theses on the church door at Wittenberg, an event that according to some modern scholars never took place – but after all, commemorations are concerned less with what actually happened than with what people believed or desired to have happened.

By the eighteenth century, celebrations of this kind had become a common practice. Among the best-known examples are the events of 1769 (the bicentenary of the birth of Shakespeare), 1788 (the centenary of the Glorious Revolution) and 1792 (the tercentenary of Columbus's discovery of the New World), examples that support the suggestion that the demand for commemoration was expanding in the later eighteenth century.[7]

In the nineteenth century, centenaries reflected what might be called the 'nationalization' of the past, a trend that is also to be seen in historiography, history painting, historical novels and elsewhere. The official or semi-official celebrations that took place in the USA in 1876 and in France in 1889 are only the most famous instances of a general trend, which also included the centenaries of national heroes such as Cervantes, Galileo and Voltaire. National consciousness also underlay the rise of anniversaries such as 4 July in the USA and 14 July in France. Hence the French historian Pascal Ory has suggested that 'plus encore qu'une territoire, une langue, une religion ou un regime, une nation, c'est une mémoire'.[8]

The study of the sociology or anthropology of commemorations goes back half a century. A landmark in this field is a book called *The Living and the Dead*, published in 1959 by the American anthropologist W. Lloyd Warner. Focussing on a place he calls 'Yankee City' (later revealed to be Newburyport in Massachusetts) Warner presented a sociological analysis of what he called the symbolic life of Americans, focussing on three forms of the performance of memory.

In the private sphere, Warner and his research assistants investigated the place of what they called 'the city of the dead', in other words the cemetery, in the family life of the citizens of Newburyport. In the public sphere, the team examined the annual observance of Memorial Day and, in particular detail, the celebration in the 1930s of the city's tercentenary, a festival that included a pageant with 42 historical tableaux. The book's message might be summed up in the paradox that commemorations of the past are really statements about the present.

One very large question raised by Warner's study is that of the relative importance of consensus and conflict in a given community. Commemorations are supposed to be performances of consensus, an agreed interpretation of the past linked to shared

---
[7] Gillis (1994).
[8] Appelbaum (1989); Spillman (1997); Ory (1992), 8.

views of the present. Like the Balinese cockfight, made famous in the academic world by Clifford Geertz, they represent a story that a given community tells itself about itself. In similar functionalist fashion, Warner had already described the Tercentenary celebrations as the story of 'what the collectivity believed and wanted itself to be'.[9]

The problem with these formulations is obvious enough. In three words: Who are 'they'? This brings us to the question of the actors, the *dramatis personae* in the theatre of memory. Is no one excluded from the memory community? Does everyone (rich and poor, male and female, old and young) tell the same story? The rituals may well be attempts to achieve consensus, identifying with the past and attempting to annihilate or deny distance or disagreement.

On the other hand, these collective performances of memory often reveal cracks or even fissures in the community. In the case of the United States in 1876, for instance, some attempts of Afro-Americans to join in the celebrations were rebuffed (although Frederick Douglas was an official guest), while the American Indians did not even offer to take part and the feminist Susan Anthony presented an unofficial Women's Declaration of Independence. For this reason scholars have coined the phrases 'counter-memory' and 'wars of memory' to refer in particular to recollections of times of conflict such the Finnish or Spanish civil wars of the twentieth century, examples recently studied by oral historians.[10]

Yankee City was not socially homogeneous either. On the contrary, like so many American cities, it was an urban mosaic of ethnic groups which had mostly arrived in the nineteenth and twentieth centuries. In the case of the tercentenary celebrations, each group sponsored a float. A problem arose when the leaders of the Jewish community were asked to sponsor a float representing Benedict Arnold, the revolutionary general who turned traitor and joined the British. In other words, whether consciously or

---

[9] Warner (1959), 107; Geertz (1973).
[10] Kammen (1991); Spillman (1997), 49, 52, 59. Davis and Starn (1989).

unconsciously, the organizers seem to have identified the traitor Arnold with Judas and Judas with the Jews. Following what Warner describes as an 'embarrassing public situation', the Jewish community were offered a different float.[11]

Another literally dramatic example of the lack of consensus, on a much grander scale, was offered by the bicentenary of the French Revolution in 1989. This occasion raised a series of dilemmas for the government of François Mitterand. Which revolution should be celebrated – the moderate revolution of 1789 or the radical revolution of 1793? Should there be a celebration at all, since a substantial minority of Frenchmen and women had opposed the Revolution? In 1989, what was called the Mission du Bicentenaire tried to emphasize harmony, while French Right organized an *Anti-89* movement, and the Communist Party's *Vive Quatre-Vingt-Neuf* stressed the social aspect of the revolution more than the official festivities were doing.

In other words, the events of 1989 commemorating the events of 1789 offer vivid examples of recurrent problems. The attempt at what Aleida Assmann calls 'national memory construction' went wrong (from the official point of view) on this occasion because different actors had their own ideas about the play to be represented.[12] Ironically enough, it was the very performance of consensus that brought the latent conflicts to the surface.

In the two case-studies from the British Isles that follow, different voices and different tunes will be heard. They deal with commemorations of seventeenth-century events in which the past has been continually reconstructed: Bonfire Night in England and in Northern Ireland the anniversaries of the battle of the Boyne and the relief of Derry. This cluster or family of performances shares a mythology in which anti-Catholicism is central, summed up in the slogan 'No Popery', a phrase which summons up a series of associated memories, ideas and emotions. All the same, in the course of this account major contrasts between the English and the Irish performances will become apparent.

---

[11] Warner (1959), 198.
[12] Ory (1992), 198-230; Kaplan (1995); cf. Garcia (2000).

Bonfire Night

5 November 1605, the day of the foiling of the attempt by Guy Fawkes and his fellow conspirators to blow up the Houses of Parliament, was officially designated a day of thanksgiving for deliverance from the plot, an early example of what has been called 'legislated memory'.[13] The festival of 5 November was soon described by an English bishop as 'our Passover' and 'our Purim'.[14]

The festival has a long but discontinuous history, with various changes or 'slippages' of meaning over the centuries. Under James I the celebrations were official. Under his successor Charles, when the Establishment in Church and State appeared to be quasi-Catholic, the celebrations became unofficial and even subversive. After the Restoration,, when Charles II was suspected (rightly, as it turns out) of being a secret Catholic, while his brother James was an open one, the bonfires again signified opposition to the regime. In the late 1670s and early 1680s, the time of the so-called 'Exclusion Crisis', the Green Ribbon Club, a Whig group, organized processions in which effigies of the pope were ceremonially burned. These processions, recorded in engravings at the time, were not exactly spontaneous and may have been early examples of 'rent-a-crowd', but it remains significant that the Whig party should have drawn on festive traditions in order to further their campaign for the exclusion of the future James II from the succession to the throne.[15]

The festival was more or less depoliticized in the eighteenth century, though in New England in 1774, the celebration, we are told, 'formed a significant part of the raising of the emotional temperature' leading to the American Revolution.[16] It was re-politicized in the early nineteenth century in response to Catholic Emancipation and the re-establishment of Catholic bishops in Britain. Thus 5 November presents a vivid example of a recurrent phenomenon, the re-activation of cultural memory

---
[13] Cressy (1992), 71.
[14] Lancelot Andrewes, quoted in Cressy (2005), 55.
[15] Jones (1956); Williams (1958); Furley (1959); Cressy (1992) 73-5; Cressy (2005), 57-61.
[16] Hastings (1997), 75.

by political events.[17] It was only in the twentieth century that Bonfire Night became 'folklore', a festival that is above all for children. As David Cressy puts it, 'Guy Fawkes Night had been tamed'.[18]

The ritual of November 5 includes an evocation of memory.

Please to remember
The fifth of November
Gunpowder, treason and plot.
I see no reason
Why gunpowder treason
Should ever be forgot.

Despite these verses the historical meaning of the festival is being forgotten, fading away, passing from the social memory into the cultural memory. Until about the 1980s one could see children displaying a rag doll in the street and asking passers-by for 'A penny for the Guy'. Today, little more than the fireworks remain in most parts of England, a display without a clear connection to a historical event, even if the quatercentenary, celebrated in 2005, was an opportunity for historians to remind the public through the media of the original meaning of the festival.

There is one major exception to this forgetfulness: the small market town of Lewes in Sussex (as well as minor exceptions in Eastbourne, Hastings and elsewhere, recent revivals on the Lewes model).[19] 5 November remains a major event in Lewes, organized by the so-called 'Bonfire Societies'. There are six bonfire societies in existence today, each with its own slice of urban territory: Cliffe, Commercial Square, Lewes Borough, Nevill Juvenile, South Street and Waterloo. The 'Bonfire Boys', as the societies used to be called – though many women now join them – organize processions through the town culminating in the burning of a number of effigies, especially that of the pope – not the current pope (though Pius IX and Leo XIII were burned in

---
[17] Cressy (2005), 61-70.
[18] Cressy (2005), 74.
[19] Etherington (1993, 1997); cf. Jay (2005), emphasizing the 1990s.

Co-memorations: Performing the past

their day), but Paul V, who was pope in 1605 – whether the choice is made out of tact or historicism or both.

Why Lewes? In some ways the town is a typical small English town, socially and politically conservative. In the nineteenth century the 'Bonfire Boys' were supporters of the monarchy and the empire. However, Lewes also has a radical tradition. 17 Protestants were burned there during the reign of Queen Mary. An anti-Catholic tradition survived into the later twentieth century. When I was living near Lewes in the 1960s and 1970s, a story circulated about a leading member of one of the bonfire societies. He was knocked down by a car and rushed to hospital. In the hospital he was asked his religion and instantly replied 'No Popery', a slogan regularly displayed on Bonfire Night. In Lewes, radical Protestantism is combined with radical politics. The radical Tom Paine lived in the town from 1768 to 1774 and his memory is still honoured there today. Unlike many small English towns, Lewes has a tradition of voting for Labour Members of Parliament.

The town's special mixture of conservatism and radicalism is reflected in the Bonfire Night ritual. The Bonfire Societies were founded in the 1850s, the result of a kind of compromise between the authorities and the organizers of unofficial celebrations, which sometimes led to riots, notably in 1847. In the nineteenth century, the societies were mainly composed of young men, often the sons of shopkeepers. By this time the upper classes, once involved, had abandoned the festival to ordinary people. They used Bonfire Night as 'a vehicle for the vilification of local figures' (the coexistence of local and national meanings for commemorations is of course important in many places besides Lewes).[20]

Today, the societies organize processions in fancy dress. Apaches, Vikings and hoplites walk through the streets and preachers condemn the pope and Guy Fawkes to the flames). There is a greater role for children than there used to be (a bonfire society has been founded especially for them, Nevill Juvenile). Vestiges of politics survive in the rituals of 5 November. Since the First World War, the societies lay wreaths at the war memorial and

---
[20] Storch (1982), 72, 76.

carry signs 'Lest We Forget'. They also burn effigies of unpopular political figures such as Mrs Thatcher or George W. Bush.[21]

It might therefore be argued that Bonfire Night in Lewes – like many other performances of the past – should be interpreted in terms of what Mikhail Bakhtin called 'heteroglossia', an event that has had different meanings for different groups of participants, some of them emphasizing tradition, others democracy and yet others popery or the carnivalesque aspect of the ritual. All the same, Bonfire Night is peripheral to English political culture. In Northern Ireland, by contrast, commemoration remains an intensely political activity and a provocation to violence.

Northern Ireland

The idea that performances of the past carry messages about the present, like the idea of conflicts of memory, could hardly be confirmed more dramatically than by examples of commemorations from Northern Ireland today.

Among the most politicized annual 'performances of memory' – a phrase used in this context by Neil Jarman in 1997 – are those that take place on 12 July, the 'glorious 12th', as participants call it.[22] On this day Protestants celebrate the anniversary of the battle of the Boyne, in which William of Orange defeated James II in 1690. The battle was actually fought on 1 July, Old Style, but the date was changed to 12 July when the Gregorian calendar was adopted in Britain, leading to the paradox of the date of an antipapal festival being calculated according to a papal calendar.

Celebrations of the victory took place in the eighteenth century but it was only in the later nineteenth century that they became regular, important and highly political events, a nice example of Eric Hobsbawm's 'invention of tradition'. The celebrations expressed what has been called 'the new unionist sense of history', arising out of political conflicts.[23] At the same time, in a manner

---
[21] Etherington (1997) figs. 44, 58 (both Cliffe).
[22] Jarman (1997).
[23] Hobsbawm and Ranger (1983); Walker (1992); Jarman (1997) 61-79.

parallel to developments in Lewes, what had been relatively undisciplined performances became less rowdy and more tightly controlled, at least for a time.

As in the case of 5 November, the meaning of the performances has changed over time. From the 1870s onwards, the parades expressed and mobilized unofficial Protestant opposition to the movement for 'Home Rule', in other words self-government for Ireland within the British Empire. In the 1920s, when Northern Ireland had its own Protestant-dominated parliament at Stormont, the parades expressed official attitudes – indeed, in 1926 the 12th was declared a public holiday. In the 1970s, however, when Northern Ireland was governed from London, the parades became once again an expression of opposition.

In other words, heteroglossia rules. 'At various times the 12th of July has been used both by and against the state, by those demanding parliamentary reform and those hostile to it, by those demanding tenant-right and those opposing it, by working class radicals and even home rulers.'[24]

Throughout the troubles in Northern Ireland from the 1960s to the present many walls have displayed the slogan 'Remember 1690', sometimes abbreviated to 'REM 1690' or accompanied by an image of William III on horseback. This is not antiquarianism, but a statement about the present couched in the language of the past. '"Remember 1690" ... is not the motto of a historical cult ... so much as the reminder of present threats to the Ulsterman's security and independence'.[25]

The evening of 11 July is a time of Fawkes-like bonfires, on which it was customary to burn an effigy of the pope (now often replaced by the tricolour of the Republic of Ireland).[26] 12 July is marked by parades organized by the lodges of the Orange Order (founded in 1795), marching in their bowler hats and sashes, and by other Protestant societies such as The Royal Black Institution. Once again, we see the importance of voluntary associations. The parades are dominated by men, although a few women march

[24] Bryan (1994), 37; cf. Bryan (2000), 7, 38, 60.
[25] Borland (2001) 279-81; Estyn Evans, quoted in Walker (1992), 13.
[26] Bryan (2000) 63, 109, 138.

and many more cheer the marchers on or sing and dance along beside them.²⁷ These performances are clearly a re-affirmation of collective identity, defined against that of the Catholics, the rival memory community. Other events besides the Boyne are also commemorated in these parades, notably the Battle of the Somme, in which the Ulster Division went into action on 1 July, allowing a conflation of the battle with that of the Boyne of the kind that is often found in myths.

The music of the flute-and-drum bands (sometimes known as 'blood and thunder' or 'kick the pope' bands) makes the performances still more dramatic and aggressive, notably the thundering of the Lambeg drums (large double-headed drums that have been used on these occasions from the 1890s onwards), and the playing of tunes such as 'The Sash my Father Wore', 'Croppies Lie Down' and 'Boyne Water', provocations to violence to which the Catholics often respond by throwing missiles at the procession. No wonder then that 12 July posers an annual problem for the government, that of deciding whether or not to allow processions and what routes the marchers should be permitted to take. The political temperature rises every July, as the 'marching season' begins. On 12 July 2005, for instance, 80 policemen were injured in Belfast alone, attempting to keep Catholics and Protestants apart when the marchers entered a Catholic zone, the Ardoyne Road to the North of the city.

A performance of memory in a still more precise sense is another festival in Northern Ireland, centred on the city known to Catholics as Derry and to Protestants as Londonderry.²⁸ To be more precise, Derry is the scene of two annual parades. What is commemorated in both cases is an event, the shutting of the gates of the city on 18 December 1688 and the relief of the siege of the city the following August. The theme of the parades along the walls of the city may be summed up in the slogan attributed to the defenders of the city: 'No Surrender'.

The two events were already celebrated in the seventeenth and

---

²⁷ Bryan (2000), 133, 142.
²⁸ McBride (1997); Fraser (2000a, 2000b).

eighteenth centuries. In 1788, for example, the centenary of the shutting of the gates (coinciding with the centenary of the Glorious Revolution) was marked by the burning in effigy of Colonel Robert Lundy, the military governor of the city who had argued that the city was indefensible and has entered the cultural memory as a traitor, the local equivalent of Guy Fawkes.[29] The burning later became an annual event. The festival of 5 November seems to have 'contaminated' 12 August as well as 12 July. In any case, traitors are prominent in the memories of many cultures, part of the emplotment of the past as a myth in which heroes and villains play key roles. This point may help explain why the citizens of Newburyport designed a float around Benedict Arnold.

All the same, as in the case of the Boyne, serious commemorations date from the nineteenth century. The organizers of the Derry parades are, once again, voluntary associations, notably the Apprentice Boys, named after the 13 apprentices who shut the gates in 1688 but founded in 1813, at a time of the movement for Catholic Emancipation (in parallel with the re-politicization of 5 November). The Boys are now divided into eight clubs, the oldest of which is the 'No Surrender' Club.[30] Incidentally, in Lewes in the 1970s, I remember seeing men in black leather jackets lettered 'No Surrender', as if 12 August had contaminated 5 November, or Ulster Protestants infiltrated a Sussex festival.

The phrase 'No Surrender' illustrates the uses of the past, transition from the siege itself to the 'siege mentality' of Ulster Protestants today. It has been a *Leitmotiv* in the fiery speeches and articles of Ian Paisley, for instance, himself a member of the Apprentice Boys. The moderate government of Terence O'Neill, in the 1960s was described by radical Protestants in terms of 'Lundyism', in other words treachery.[31] The myth of an embattled but pure community coexists with a messier reality of power-sharing and everyday social interactions across the cultural frontier.

As in the case of 12 July, the route taken by the marchers is a matter of political importance, since Derry is now a divided city

[29] McBride (1997) 17, 41.
[30] McBride (1997), 38, 47, 49.
[31] Cooke (1996), 159, 174, 177; McBride (1997), 73.

with a majority of Catholics in an area called the Bogside (below the old walls), and confrontations are not uncommon, notably in 1969, when riots lasted for three days and ushered in thirty years of what the Irish call 'troubles'. In recent years, by contrast, Catholics and Protestants have been working together to turn 12 August into a more inclusive occasion.[32]

Both performances may be described as examples of 'construction', the construction of identity via the construction of the past. The problem is that in Northern Ireland the same space – and the same past – is shared by two nations, the orange nation and the green nation, with rival interpretations of the past, views of the present and hopes for the future.

To conclude, it may be useful to reflect on the metaphor of 'performance'. These commemorations take place on a 'stage', in particular locations in Lewes, Derry Belfast and elsewhere – in our age of globalization, Orangemen also march in Accra on 12 July.[33] In the Northern Irish case the term 'arena' is even more appropriate. These places evoke rival memories and easily turn into battlegrounds.

What of the actors?[34] The main actors in these performances are collective, voluntary associations such as the Bonfire Societies, the Orange Order and the No Surrender Club. Voluntary associations often play a leading role in the organization of collective performances, from medieval guilds to the Green Ribbon Club in seventeenth-century London and the *escolas de samba* in the Carnival of Río de Janeiro today. However, the gap between audience and spectators is a narrow one. Many spectators participate, in the Northern Irish case by attacking or defending the marchers. The sharpest line is not between performers and spectators but between the immediate spectators, present on stage, and the remote spectators, viewing the marches on television or in the photographs in the next day's newspaper. Even the remote spectators have their memories re-activated or shaped by what they see on the screen.

[32] Ross (2007)117-21.
[33] McGrath (1999).
[34] Cf. Ory (1992), 19-43.

Co-memorations: Performing the past

Is there or isn't there a script for these performances? Yes, in the sense that there is a good deal of repetition, and that participants act on their memories of past performances. No, in the sense that there is always room for improvisation, to say nothing of the event going 'wrong' in the sense of turning out different from expectations. Hence historians need to adopt the method the French call *histoire sérielle*, studying the performances in chronological order with eyes open for both repetition and variation.

These performances have no director and even on the same occasion different actors may have somewhat different aims. Commemorations, like other festivals, used to be studied as performances of consensus, as in the case of the studies by Warner and Geertz. By contrast, the last generation of historians and anthropologists alike has placed more emphasis on heteroglossia and the conflicting interpretations of participants in the 'same' performance.[35] This approach is an appropriate one, as we have seen, to the case of Bonfire Night and still more to the Northern Irish commemorations.[36]

All the same, an exclusive preoccupation with the multiplicity of voices in a performance may miss something important. To Bakhtin's concept of heteroglossia we need to add his concept of dialogue. In their performances as in their everyday life, the Catholics and the Protestants of Northern Ireland engage in dialogue. It might be described as a dialogue of the deaf, of the kind represented in Pinter's plays, but it is a form of dialogue nevertheless. The point is that Catholics and Protestants respond to each other's performances, by imitation or adaptation as well as by violence. Orange and Green are like Siamese twins. They define their identities against each other ('Micks' versus 'Prods'). The Orange Lodges have their complementary opposite in the Ancient Order of Hibernians, which also parades through the streets. The two nations share a mythologized past, even if one reconstruction is the mirror image of the other, the heroes and villains reversed. Latent in everyday life, the annual performances

---
[35] Guss (2000).
[36] Buchanan (2005) 7, 51-2, 59, 61.

make these rival images manifest and open old wounds. They dramatize memory wars that also exist elsewhere, in Finland, for instance, and in Spain. They are the scene of memories of conflict that are also conflicts of memory.

Bibliography

Diana K. Appelbaum (1989) *The Glorious Fourth*, New York.

A. Assmann (1999) *Erinnerungsräume: Formen und Wandlungen des kulturellen Gedächtnisses*, Munich.

John Borland (2001) 'Graffit, Paraden und Alltagskultur in Nordirland', in Harald Welzer (ed.) *Das Soziale Gedächtnis: Geschichte, Erinnerung, Tradierung*, Hamburg, 276-95.

Dominic Bryan (1994) 'Interpreting the 12$^{th'}$, *History Ireland* 2, 37-41.

Dominic Bryan (2000) *Orange Parades.*

A. D. Buckley and Mary C. Kenney (1995) *Negotiating Identity: Rhetoric, Metaphor and Social Drama in Northern Ireland*, Washington.

Brenda Buchanan et al. (2005) *Gunpowder Plots*, London.

Denis Cooke (1996) *Persecuting Zeal*, Dingle.

David Cressy (1989) *Bonfires and Bells: National Memory and the Protestant Calendar in Elizabethan and Stuart England*, Berkeley CA.

David Cressy (1992) 'The 5th of November Remembered', in Roy Porter (ed.) *Myths of the English*, Cambridge, 68-90.

David Cressy (2005) 'Five Hundred Years of Festivities', in Buchanan et al., 49-79.

Jean Davallon, Philippe Dujardin and Gérard Sabatier (1993) *Politique de la mémoire*, Lyon.

Natalie Z. Davis and Randolf Starn (1989, eds.) Memory and Counter-Memory, *Representations* 26.

Jim Etherington (1978) 'The Lewes Bonfire Riots of 1847', *Sussex History* 1.

J. Etherington (1993) *Lewes Bonfire Night*, Seaford.

T. G. Fraser (ed., 2000a) *The Irish Parading Tradition.*

T. G. Fraser (2000b) 'The Apprentice Boys and the Relief of Derry Parades', in *The Irish Parading Tradition*, 173-90.

O. W. Furley (1959) 'The Pope-Burning Processions of the Late 17th Century', *History* 44, 16-23.

Patrick Garcia (2000) *Le bicentenaire de la Révolution française. Pratiques sociales d'une commémoration*, Paris.

John Gillis (1994) 'Memory and Identity: the History of a Relationship', in Gillis (ed.) *Commemorations: the Politics of National Identity*, Princeton NJ, 3-24.

David M. Guss (2000) *The Festive State: Race, Ethnicity and Nationalism as Cultural Performance*, Berkeley etc.

Adrian Hastings (1997) *The Construction of Nationhood: Ethnicity, Religion and Nationalism*, Cambridge.

Eric Hobsbawm and Terence Ranger (eds., 1983) *The Invention of Tradition*, Cambridge.

Neil Jarman (1997) *Material Conflicts: Parades and Visual Displays in Northern Ireland*, Oxford.

Mike Jay (2005) 'Bonfire Night in Lewes', in Buchanan et al., 118-44.

James R. Jones (1956) 'The Green Ribbon Club', *Durham University Journal* 49, 17-20.

Michael Kammen (1991) *Mystic Chords of Memory: the transformation of tradition in American culture*, New York.

Steven Kaplan (1995) *Farewell, Revolution*, 2 vols., Ithaca NY.

Alison Landsberg (2004) *Prosthetic Memory: the transformation of American remembrance in the age of mass culture*, New York.

Sidsel Saugestad Larsen (1982) 'The Glorious 12th: the Politics of Legitimation in Kilbroney', in *Belonging: identity and social organization in British Rural Cultures*, ed. Anthony P. Cohen, Manchester, 278-91.

Joep Leerssen (1996) *Remembrance and Imagination*, Cork.

Ian McBride (1997) *The Siege of Derry in Ulster Protestant Mythology*, Dublin.

Ian McBride (ed., 2001) *History and Memory in Modern Ireland*, Cambridge.

Chris McGrath (1999) 'Ulster-by-the-Equator', *The Guardian*, 6 November.

Pascal Ory (1992) *Une nation pour mémoire*, Paris.

Roy Rosenzweig and David Thelen (1998) *The Presence of the Past*, New York.

Marc H. Ross (2007) *Cultural Contestation in Ethnic Conflict*, Cambridge.

John H. M. Salmon (1959) *The French Wars in English Political Thought*, Oxford.

James Sharpe (2005) *Remember, Remember: a cultural history of Guy Fawkes' Day*, Cambridge MA.

Lyn Spillman (1997) *Nation and Commemoration: Creating National Identities in the United States and Australia*, Cambridge.

Robert D. Storch (1982) 'Please to Remember the 5th of November: Conflict, Solidarity and Public Order in Southern England, 1815-1900', in Storch (ed.) *Popular Culture and Custom in 19th-Century England*, London, 71-99.

Diana Taylor (2003) *The Archive and the Repertoire: Performing Cultural Memory in the Americas*, Durham NC.

Brian Walker (1992) '1641, 1689, 1690 and All That: the unionist sense of history', revised version in *Dancing to History's Tune: history, myth and politics in Ireland*, Belfast 1996, 1-14.

W. Lloyd Warner (1959) *The Living and the Dead*.

Sheila Williams (1958) 'The Pope-Burning Processions of 1679-81', *Journal of the Warburg and Courtauld Institutes* 21, 104-18.

7: THE DIRECTOR AS HISTORIAN: ROSSELLINI'S LOUIS XIV

'Film should be a means like any other, perhaps more valuable than any other, of writing history' (Rossellini).

In this chapter, I should like to look at Rossellini and his *Prise de pouvoir par Louis XIV* (1966) as if the director were a historian of the king's reign. I say 'as if he were a historian', not to exclude him from the guild (in my view anyone who does history is a historian, whatever trade union they happen to belong to), but simply to leave open the question whether Rossellini was using the past as an allegory of the present or reflecting in general terms on the nature of power. My own view, though, is that Rossellini was also doing history. He is a distinguished exemplar of what the American critic Hayden White calls 'historiophoty', defined as 'the representation of history and our thought about it in visual images and filmic discourse'.[1] After all, this was the director who declared that 'Film should be a means like any other, perhaps more valuable than any other, of writing history'.[2] *La prise de pouvoir* comes in the later part of Rossellini's

---

[1] Hayden V. White, 'Historiography and Histroiophoty', *American Historical Review* 93 (1988), 1193-99.
[2] Claude Beylie, 'Brève rencontre avec Roberto Rossellini' *Ecran* 34 (1975).

career, when he was sixty and had made his didactic turn, which was also a historical turn.³

The reasons for the turn are briefly explained in the *Manifesto* (1965) which Bertolucci and others also signed, arguing that their aim in cinema and TV should be to show their audiences the main trends of human history, or as the manifesto puts it more vividly, 'to show to humanity the conducting wires of their history [*proporre a l'uomo i fili conduttori della sua storia*].⁴ The series of historical films he made in order to do this begins with 'The Iron Age' [*L'età del ferro*, 1964], 'Man's Struggle for Survival' [*La lotta dell'uomo per la sua sopravivenza*, 1964-70], and films about Descartes, Pascal, Socrates, Augustine, the Acts of the Apostles and the age of Cosimo de'Medici. In the case of the film about Louis, the commission from French television liberated Rossellini from the pressures of the box-office.

In what follows I shall examine *La prise de pouvoir par Louis XIV*, from the point of view of the historian's two main tasks, in the first place the imaginative recreation of the past, and in the second place its interpretation. This will involve a discussion of Rossellini's sources and his use of them, of his sense of history (especially social history) and finally his views of Louis XIV and the significance of his reign.

Rossellini's Sources

'Gruault got the documents together for me, with Philippe Erlanger as the historical adviser'.⁵ What documents? The text of La Rochefoucauld's *Maximes*, from which Louis is shown reading at the end of the film; the famous memoirs of the Duc de

---

³ Among the earlier studies of this film, I am particularly indebted to James R. MacBean, 'Rossellini's Materialist Mise-en-Scène of *La prise de pouvoir de Louis XIV*', *Film Quarterly* 25 (1971-2), no. 2, 20-9; Peter Brunette, *Roberto Rossellini* (New York, 1987); Gianni Rondolino, *Roberto Rossellini* (Turin, 1989); Peter Bondanella, *The Films of Roberto Rossellini* (Cambridge, 1993); Tag Gallagher, *The Adventures of Roberto Rossellini* (New York, 1998).
⁴ Quoted in Rondolino, *Rossellini*.
⁵ Rossellini in Beylie, 'Brève rencontre'.

Saint-Simon, which offer the fullest and most vivid descriptions of the court rituals that Rossellini presents so memorably on the screen; and probably Louis's 'memoirs' as well. Ghost-written by secretaries and intended not for publication but for the education of the Dauphin, the memoirs are of great value for the reconstruction of the king's self-image and the image which he wished others to have of him. On the other hand, there does not seem to have been any use of two important sources. Had Rossellini known of La Bruyère's description of the chapel at Versailles, with the courtiers, their backs to the altar, adoring their earthly god the king, he would surely have been unable to resist it. The same point might be made about the memoirs of the Italian nobleman Primi Visconti, which offer vivid details which fit in very well with Rossellini's image of the theatre of the court. Visconti claims to have glimpsed the king as he crossed the threshold between his private rooms and the public part of Versailles, and saw him standing up straight and preparing to play the role of king.[6]

Of course a film director would draw not only on texts but on visual sources as well, the Palace of Versailles, for example. Rossellini clearly used paintings and engravings of Louis and the main figures of his court, since the way in which Jean-Baptiste Colbert, for example, is presented in the film follows these sources quite closely. It is also clear that Rossellini could not resist using or alluding to some famous nineteenth-century images of the age of Louis, from *Les trois mousquetaires* of Dumas (from whom he borrows D'Artagnan) to the painting by Paul Delaroche, *Cardinal Mazarin Mourant*, the model for part of the famous death-bed scene. Another nineteenth-century image of Louis, which we owe to William Thackeray, will be discussed below.[7]

As we have seen, Rossellini was advised by a historian, and the credits at the start of the film say 'Scénario de Philippe Erlanger.' Erlanger, who had published a biography of Louis in 1965, just in time to be used by Rossellini, was quite well-known at the time

[6] Primi Visconti, *Mémoires sur la cour de Louis XIV, 1673-1681*, ed. Jean-François Solnon (Paris, 1988).
[7] Stephen Bann, *Paul Delaroche* (London, 1997), 67.

as a writer of popular works of history, concentrating on royal biographies (Henri III, Louis XIII, and so on). His study of Louis was not specially original or distinguished but it presented the conventional wisdom in a fluent, clear and accessible form.[8]

An examination of the text leaves little room for doubt that Rossellini studied a few pages of Erlanger (pp. 101-14) with care when creating the script of the film, and other parts of the book are also used occasionally. It may be revealing to study what was borrowed, what was rejected and how what was borrowed was transformed, in the way in which Shakespeare scholars examine his use of the historian Saxo Grammaticus in *Hamlet*. For example, the scenes of Mazarin and the doctors, Mazarin and his confessor, and the offer of a bequest which the king refuses are all in this section of Erlanger, while the quarrel between Louis and his mother draws on a later passage of the biography.[9]

The famous statement that the king would govern by himself and that 'not even a passport' was to be issued without his permission is taken from Erlanger's quotation of it.[10] Rossellini took comments by Erlanger to the effect that 'No French king had taken power at his accession for 200 years' and that 'at the age of 20, François I thought only of battles', and put them into the mouth of Louis' mother, Anne of Austria.[11]

Some dramatic incidents recounted by Erlanger are omitted. In the film we see the arrest of the financier Nicholas Fouquet in some detail, but not the famous festival at his château of Vaux-le-Vicomte to which he invited the king and the court (it has often been suggested that the magnificence of the entertainment, too splendid for a mere subject, was the reason for Fouquet's downfall). On the other hand, an event mentioned only briefly in Erlanger is sometimes given prominence by Rossellini. The incident in which Fouquet tries to bribe La Vallière is linked to the financier's arrest in the film but not in the book.[12] A brief quotation

---

[8] Philippe Erlanger, *Louis XIV* (Paris, 1965).
[9] Erlanger, *Louis*, 134.
[10] Erlanger, *Louis*, 109.
[11] Erlanger, *Louis*, 104.
[12] Erlanger, *Louis*, 113-4.

from the Venetian ambassador about cloaks for courtiers designed by the king forms the basis of the famous scene of the king and the tailor, in which Louis expresses his ideas about the proper costume for courtiers.[13]

In a way it is a pity that Rossellini did not make the film a year later. In that case he would have been able to use another study of the king, Pierre Goubert's *Louis XIV et vingt millions de Français* (1966). Goubert, a leading historian of the so-called '*Annales* School', was a specialist on the French peasants. His account of the king's reign is an unusual one, more critical of Louis than most of his predecessors and more concerned with the social effects of his policies. However, it might be argued that Rossellini did not need to consult Goubert's book precisely because, like the author, he was interested in everyday life and ordinary people.

The History of the Everyday

The film historian and film theorist Siegfried Kracauer once claimed in a letter to the art historian Erwin Panofsky that a study of German films would reveal something about German life that other sources could not. 'The whole dimension of everyday life with its infinitesimal movements and its multitude of transitory actions could be disclosed nowhere but on the screen ... films illuminate the realm of bagatelles, of little events'.[14] A concern with the history of the everyday is now common, but it was rare in 1966, when Kracauer was writing (Fernand Braudel's famous study of the subject appeared only in 1967).[15]

Rossellini got there first. *Louis XIV* begins with an invented scene of ordinary people gossiping on the banks of the river when the doctors arrive to attend Mazarin. The film emphasises everyday work, the anonymous labour of ordinary people and its contribution to cultural reproduction or to what we call 'history',

---
[13] Erlanger, *Louis*, 142.
[14] Volker Breidecker (ed.) Siegfried Kracauer/Erwin Panofsky, *Briefwechsel* (Berlin, 1966), 16.
[15] Fernand Braudel, *Civilisation matérielle et capitalisme* (Paris, 1967).

as if Rossellini were consciously answering' the famous questions asked by Brecht's worker.[16] In this respect it is reminiscent of the slightly earlier Russian *Hamlet* directed by Grigori Kozintsev (1963). We see Versailles, for instance, not only as a finished product, an environment for the king, but under construction by a whole army of masons, bricklayers and carpenters.

Again, we see the grand royal meals not only from above, where Louis is eating them, but also 'from below' (the slogan of the left-wing historians of the sixties), from the kitchen where they are being prepared. The juxtaposition of these opposite viewpoints deserves to be noted. The complex social hierarchy of the court is shown by means of the relaying of orders down the social scale. The attention given to animals, especially dogs, indoors as well as out-of-doors, rings true to historians of the seventeenth century.[17]

The materiality of Rossellini's films has often been discussed (for example by MacBean), who compares him to the Marxist archaeologist Gordon Childe. In *Louis XIV*, material objects are sometimes a focus of attention, from Mazarin's chamber pot to the covered dish of pork presented to the king. There is even a discussion in the film of Louis' objections to forks, suggesting that Rossellini – or one of his advisers – had been reading the famous study of the history of table manners by the German sociologist Norbert Elias.[18]

The ritualization of the everyday life of the court is a recurrent motif in the film, the *cortège* forming to escort 'la viande du roi', the royal *lever* and so on. Rossellini wants his viewers not only to see but also to understand what appears to be strange, as if the past were a 'foreign country' and the director a historical anthropologist. Hence his employment, more than once in the course of the film, of the traditional device of the outsider who asks questions – why does the queen clap her hands in the royal bedchamber? Why does the king not enter the room in which the body of Mazarin is lying in state?

---

[16] Bertolt Brecht, 'Fragen eines lesenden Arbeiters'.
[17] Cf. Keith Thomas, *Man and the Natural World* (London, 1983).
[18] Norbert Elias, *Über den Prozeß der Zivilisation* (Basel, 1939). The French translation did not appear until 1973.

Rossellini's Louis

Treating Rossellini as a fellow-historian, and his film as if it were a book about Louis which has arrived for review, it is time to engage with his interpretation of the man and the reign, criticizing it or qualifying it in some respects and supporting it in others. To sum up this interpretation in a few words: Rossellini's Louis is short, heavy and rather unprepossessing but he is decisive, and he has revolutionary intentions. He aims at nothing less than the modernization of France, putting an end to noble power and disorder.

To present his interpretation of the reign, Rossellini focusses on a single moment, the moment of the king's seizure of power in 1661, a kind of *coup d'état*. Or to speak more exactly, he shows us a long moment of six or seven months beginning in February 1661 with the illness of the cardinal, showing us the death of Mazarin and the declaration of personal rule (March) and moving on to the arrest of Nicholas Fouquet in September. It is not altogether clear how much later the final scene in the film is supposed to take place – Louis looks somewhat older in that scene and since he holds a printed copy of the maxims of La Rochefoucauld, first published in 1665, the film should really refer to that year or later.

In my opinion, Rossellini was essentially right in his portrayal of the situation in 1661, emphasizing the fear that disorders might recur. The people shown on the river-bank at the beginning of the film are talking about the execution of Charles I in 1649, while Louis speaks to his mother about his memories of the rebellion known as the 'Fronde', also from the late 1640s. The point about Louis and his memories of the Fronde is a commonplace one, but the emphasis on the king's desire for order and fear of disorder is Rossellini's point rather than Erlanger's and it is to my mind convincing as history as well as drama. The long reign and the achievement of 'absolute power', which in retrospect looks virtually inevitable, could not be taken for granted in 1661.

On the other hand, I think that Rossellini exaggerates the role and the greatness of Louis XIV. This was the appropriate interpretation for French television to present in the age of Charles de Gaulle, but it is difficult not to speculate about Rossellini's own attitudes, whether his Louis represents his dream of a decisive leader who would modernize and bring order to an Italy which – even in the sixties, when the 'economic miracle' was under way – was backward and chaotic in important respects.

It may be useful to distinguish five problems in this interpretation of the king and the reign, an interpretation which is not, it should be emphasized, unique to Rossellini but one that he takes over and makes his own.

a) Most of the time, Louis is presented to us giving orders rather than taking advice (though he does give Colbert a chance to expound his vision of the future). The role of ministers is downplayed.

b) The royal decisions are presented as breaches with tradition, although the *lever, couvert* and other court rituals were actually traditional rituals that were elaborated by the king and his advisers in the course of the reign.[19]

c) The decisions appear to be planned in advance rather than as responses to circumstances. For example, Rossellini's Louis declares that 'I shall establish myself in Versailles', in 'the temple of the monarchy', and Versailles appears almost immediately in its present form, as if by a miracle. In fact the conversion of Versailles from a royal hunting-lodge to the residence of the court was spread over more than twenty years, 1661-83, and some rebuilding was necessary, given the changes of plan.[20] It is somewhat ironic that a director who liked his actors to improvise does not seem to want to admit that the real Louis also improvised.

d) The idea that the king attempted to weaken the nobility is a half-truth, something of an exaggeration. Over the last generation

---

[19] Peter Burke, *The Fabrication of Louis XIV* (New Haven CN, 1992).
[20] Guy Walton, *Louis XIV's Versailles* (Harmondsworth, 1986).

or so, historians have come to emphasize the king's co-operation with the nobles.[21]

In any case, Rossellini's Louis is too modern, despite his traditional ambition to keep people in their place. Anachronisms are put into his mouth, such as 'opinion publique' (an eighteenth-century term), and he is made to refer too frequently and too sympathetically to 'mon peuple' (he did this at the time of the famine of 1709, but there is little earlier evidence of what we might call a social conscience).

e) Focussing on 1661, Rossellini gives the impression that what Louis wanted is what actually happened. We don't see the later years of the reign, so we don't see whether the king's 'revolution' worked, leaving the audience to assume that it did. We don't see the king's wars, including serious defeats. We don't see resistance to his orders by Protestants, peasants and others. There is an unresolved tension between Rossellini's interpretation of French society, in which he emphasizes what is traditional and what is alien to us, and his interpretation of the king's reign, in which what he says is effectively that Louis arrived – *enfin Louis vint* – that he saw what was wrong with France and then gave orders that changed the world.

It might of course be argued that the focus on 1661 is a response to the exigencies of film, something like the doctrine of the unity of time in the French theatre of Louis' day (with six months in the place of twenty-four hours).[22] Nonetheless there is no reason why a film about Louis could not have shown scenes from different decades of the reign had the director wanted. In short, there are many criticisms to make, which might be summed up by saying that Rossellini swallows – or uses for his own purposes – the myth of control, omniscience ('informé de tout') and virtual omnipotence, projected in the *Memoirs* of the king.

---

[21] William Beik, *Louis XIV and Absolutism* (Boston MA, 2000).
[22] Bondanella, *Rossellini*.

The Theatre of Power

So far as one major theme is concerned, however, it is difficult not to agree with Rossellini, and that is his visual discussion of the theatre of power. The director was concerned with the king's self-presentation long before historians (myself included) took up this topic.[23] Rossellini found a perfect theme for historiophoty: the politics of spectacle. 'My basic idea', as he explained in an interview, was that Louis had changed the world through a change of style, dress and etiquette'. He makes it the king's plan to govern through appearances.

The idea of the 'theatre' of power is not anachronistic – quite the opposite. The contrast between reality and appearance, *être* and *paraître* was frequently made in the seventeenth century, in the maxims of La Rochefoucauld and elsewhere. Contemporaries liked to repeat the adage that 'all the world's a stage'. Some parts of the world were seen as more of a stage than others. the court in particular. As Queen Elizabeth once remarked, 'we princes ... are set on stages'. Saint-Simon uses theatrical metaphors to refer to the court of Louis. The officially-inspired memoirs of the king emphasize the impression of magnificence and power given by the festival staged in 1662, the *carrousel*, including mock-battles in which the king took part.

Peter Bondanella, who has written on Machiavelli as well as on Rossellini, compares the techniques of governing through appearances shown in *La prise de pouvoir* with those recommended in *Il principe*. It should be added Louis probably knew the ideas of Machiavelli via Cardinal Mazarin.[24] However, Rossellini has the advantage over historians who write texts of being able to use spectacle to analyse spectacle, to *show* this policy in action, Mazarin rouging his face and Louis designing clothes. The slow and stately pace of the scenes of court ritual and the relative lack of words (in contrast, say, to Rossellini's *L'età di Cosimo de'*

---

[23] Jean-Marie Apostolides, *Le roi-machine: spectacle et politique au temps de Louis XIV* (Paris, 1981); Louis Marin, *Le Portrait du Roi* (Paris, 1981); Burke, *Fabrication*.

[24] Bondanella, *Rossellini*; cf. Paul Sonnino, 'The Sun King's "Anti-Machiavel"', in John Rule (ed.) *Louis XIV and the Craft of Kingship* (Columbus OH, 1964), 345-61.

Medici) emphasises the point. So it is odd that it was missed by the political scientist Pierre Schwartzenberg, whose book on the 'theatre state' was published in 1977, makes television responsible for the rise of the 'star system' in politics, as if he were unaware of Rossellini's film and did not realise that the sun king too had been a star.[25]

In the final scene Rossellini takes his viewers behind the scenes. I should like to suggest that this scene has a visual source, the novelist William Thackeray's engraving showing three images of the king and his clothes: first the magnificent costume, then little old man with his bald head and knock knees, and finally the combination of the two into Hyacinthe Rigaud's famous state portrait of the king in his coronation robes.[26] However, Rossellini uses the motif of undressing for a different purpose, not satirically as in Thackeray but more sympathetically, to show that Louis was mortal like the rest of us and also that he was aware of his mortality.

---

[25] Pierre Rosenberg, *L'état-spectacle: essai sur et contre le star system en politique* (Paris, 1977).
[26] William Thackeray, *Paris Sketchbook* (London, 1840): https://commons.wikimedia.org/.../File:1840_engraving_depicting_Louis_XIV_of_Fr...

8: THE RECONSTRUCTION OF POLITICAL RITUALS IN THE AGE OF LOUIS XIV

This paper is divided into four parts, moving from the small-scale to the large-scale and from the particular to the general. The first part begins with a story, with the micro-history of a small and apparently trivial incident. The second part of the paper attempts to place this incident in a broader context, the context of what I believe to be a conscious programme for the 'reconstruction' of political rituals in the age of Louis XIV. The third part is concerned with the place of this period in the history of diplomatic protocol. Finally, I shall offer a few general reflections on political ritual and 'political theatre'.

The study of political rituals is a well-established field within social anthropology.[1] However, it is well known that political historians resisted anthropology longer than their colleagues in social and cultural history. I can still remember introducing a historian of diplomacy to a social anthropologist in Canberra in 1983, and the surprise on the face of the historian when the anthropologist (Bernard Cohn) asked her about the rituals of diplomacy.

---

[1] Georges Balandier, *L'anthropologie politique* (Paris, 1967): David L. Kertzer, *Ritual, Politics and Power* (New Haven, 1988).

In the last few years, the situation has changed. A major study of the congress of Utrecht published in 1990 by Lucien Bely (originally a doctoral thesis supervised by Daniel Roche), is, among other things a response to the challenge of historical anthropology. My contribution today is another response to the challenge, though it is a relatively slight one, an 'essay' in every sense of the term as well as a complement to my recent book on the image of Louis XIV. It is on Louis that this paper will focus, leaving Louis XIII and Godefroy to Michèle Fogel.

1. The brawl in London, 1661

To begin with the micro-history. In London, on 30 September 1661, there occurred what would now be called a diplomatic 'incident'. It was a conflict over precedence which developed into a public brawl. The protagonists of this conflict were Charles baron de Vatteville, a noble from Besançon who had recently been appointed Spanish ambassador to the court of King Charles II, and the French ambassador to the same court, the Comte d'Estrades. The occasion was the arrival of the Swedish ambassador to present his credentials. The presentation of credentials was already in the late seventeenth century a ritualized occasion in which the diplomatic corps took part, with a cortège of carriages.

It was in the course of this cortège, in Whitehall that the vehicles of the French and Spanish ambassadors both attempted to take the first place. The result was of course a traffic accident, which in turn escalated into what a contemporary called a 'fray', in other words a brawl between the servants of Watteville and Estrades. Two English diarists who lived in London at the time, John Evelyn and Samuel Pepys, both recorded the details of the incident with malicious pleasure.[2]

The London brawl is well-known, but it has not yet been taken seriously enough by historians. Conflicts over precedence were of course endemic during the old regime. Modern historians

---
[2] Samuel Pepys, *Diary*, ed. Robin Latham and W. Matthews, 12 vols, London 1970-83: John Evelyn, *Diary*, ed. E. S. de Beer (5 vols, Oxford, 1955).

used to dismiss these conflicts as trivial, childish or laughable, but they now take them more seriously and interpret them more anthropologically as concrete illustrations of the importance of the principle of hierarchy in the social system of the period, a hierarchy which was expressed in concrete form in the many public processions of the period.³

This particular diplomatic incident is unusually rich in political significance, since it involved the representatives of two powers each of which considered itself – despite the survival of the Empire – the first in Europe. Whether Vatteville and Estrades were aware of this or not, a similar conflict between the Spanish and the French ambassadors (Gondomar and Marets) had taken place in London more than forty years earlier, in 1618. Again, in Rome in 1647, the French ambassador refused to receive cardinal Savelli because he had visited the Spanish ambassador first.⁴

However, the 1661 incident stands out from others in its consequences. It was reported in the *Gazette* a few days later, under the heading 'De Londres, 20 Octobre'. The anonymous author of the report assumes that the audience already knows the details, and simply comments on 'l'étonnement qu'y a laissé l'emportement que les Espagnols firent paroître en cette recontre, pour une chose dont les François sont en possession depuis si longtemps'.⁵ The Comte de Brienne, who reported the incident to Louis XIV, recorded the king's furious reaction, and quotes him as declaring that he would force Philip IV 'à céder à mes ambassadeurs la préséance dans toutes les cours de l'Europe'.⁶

For a fuller expression of Louis' point of view, we may turn to the royal memoirs, produced by his secretaries a few years later for the education of the Dauphin. This short text devotes no fewer than eight pages to the incident in London, claiming that it was no accident but 'une résolution faite de longue main', and that Vatteville 'avoit prétendu former une concurrence de rang entre

---

³ Robert Darnton, ` A bourgeois puts his world in order', in his *The Great Cat Massacre* (New York, 1984), ch. 3.
⁴ François de Callières, *De la manière de negocier avec les souverains* (Brussels, 1716), 92.
⁵ *Gazette* (1661) 1154-5.
⁶ L. – H. de Loménie, comte de Brienne, *Mémoires* (3 vols, Paris 1919), 1, 102.

les ministres du roi son maître et les miens', using for the purpose 'une troupe de canaille armée'.[7]

The end of the affair was a Spanish apology. As the *Gazette* tells the story, 'De Paris, 1 Avril 1662', the Spanish ambassador to the court of Louis XIV, the count of Fuentes, went to the Louvre and presented a letter from his master Philip IV, 'pour réparation de l'attentat du Baron de Batteville' (sic), instructing his ambassadors not to compete for precedence with their French colleagues. 'Comme cette déclaration était de grande importance', Louis XIV summoned thirty members of the diplomatic corps as witnesses of his victory.[8]

2. The reconstruction of political rituals in France, 1661-1715

What was the significance of this event? The collision between the two carriages was clearly no accident. It was a step in a ritualized affirmation of the position of France as the dominant power in Europe, soon after Louis XIV took the decision to rule by himself. The meaning of the ritual becomes clearer if we place it in the context of other events of the 1660s, or more exactly other battles between the King of France and other rulers fought in the field of protocol.

For example, there was the conflict between France and England over the so-called 'différend du pavillon', in other words the question of naval salutes, which was solved or shelved by instructions to the navies of both sides to avoid meeting each other.[9] Again, there was the affair of the Corsican guards in Rome in 1662, when Louis claimed that his representative had been insulted and demanded an apology from the pope, which he received in 1664. Given this trend, it looks as if Louis' accusation against Spain that the 1661 incident was 'une résolution faite de longue main' should be turned the other way to apply to France.

---
[7] Louis XIV, *Mémoires*, ed. Jean Longnon (Paris 1927), 90-8.
[8] *Gazette* (1662), 305-6.
[9] Pierre Goubert, *L'avènement du roi soleil* (Paris, 1967), 146-7.

The Reconstruction of Political Rituals in the Age of Louis XIV

I have no document to support this hypothesis, and in any case the important point is not the origin of the brawl, but its consequences. For the French government, the incidents in London and Rome did not end with the apologies. On the contrary, these French victories in the field of ritual were recorded and celebrated in various ways. The defeat of Spain was marked by the striking of medals with inscriptions *Jus Praecedendi Assertum*, and *Loco et Dignitate cedit Hispanus*. In similar fashion, the humbling of the pope was followed by the erection of a pyramid and the striking of a medal inscribed *Corsici Facinoris Excusatio*. The medals were later reproduced in the medallic histories of the reign compiled by Menestrier and by the Académie des Inscriptions, in the latter case combined with an official narrative of the two incidents.[10]

One of the few historians to have taken the London brawl seriously, William Roosen, has discussed it from the point of view of a 'systems approach' to early modern diplomatic ceremonial, treating ceremonial as a 'barometer' of changes in international relations, in other words as the cultural expression – or we might say the 'dramatization' – of changes which had already occurred.[11]

The point of view from which this paper was written, however, is closer to that of the anthropologists, particularly those who have studied ritual as 'social drama' (in the famous phrase of Victor Turner) or as 'performance'. In her study of the Wolof, for instance, Judith Irvine has noted the way in which a ritualized encounter, for example a greeting, can be manipulated by one party to establish dominance over the other.[12]

In other words, ritual, like other forms of communication, is a means to make change occur. In the case with which we are

---

[10] C. F. Menestrier, *Histoire de Louis le Grand par les médailles* (Paris, 1691), nos. 69, 78; Josèphe Jacquiot, *Médailles et jetons de Louis XIV* (4 vols, Paris, 1968), 158ff, 168.

[11] William Roosen, 'Early Modern Diplomatic Ceremonial: a Systems Approach', *Journal of Modern History* 52 (1980), 452-76.

[12] Victor Turner, *The Drums of Affliction* (Oxford, 1968), ch. 4; Judith Irvine, 'Strategies of Status Manipulation in the Wolof Greeting', in *Explorations in the Ethnography of Speaking*, ed. Richard Bauman and Joel Sherzer (Cambridge,1974), 167-91; cf Anne Salmond, 'Rituals of Encounter among the Maori', *ibid.*, 192-21.

concerned, ritual was used to make certain moves in the 'Great Game' of diplomacy. We might describe these conflicts over ritual as continuations of warfare by other means.[13] Or as a form of 'cold war' preceding formal hostilities (the War of Devolution between France and Spain began in 1667, six years after the London brawl).

The central hypothesis put forward in this paper is that Louis XIV and his advisers, notably Jean-Baptiste Colbert, were not only well aware of the political importance of ritual but that they were also putting into practice a carefully thought-out plan for its reconstruction.

This hypothesis is supported by a notorious incident from the year 1684. When the government of the city-state of Genoa permitted the construction of galleys for the Spanish navy, the city was bombarded into submission by a French fleet and a special ritual of humiliation was invented for the occasion. The doge of Genoa was required to visit Versailles, accompanied by four senators, *faire des soumissions au Roy*, making a speech of apology in which he removed his hat every time he mentioned the name of Louis. Like the brawl in Whitehall and the affair of the Corsican guards, this incident was commemorated by a medal, inscribed *Genua Obsequens*, as well as in tapestries. A painting was commissioned from Claude Hallé in which Louis is represented standing on the steps of his throne while the doge bows low before him.[14]

The diplomatic incidents I have described are clearly insufficient in themselves to justify the claim that there was a 'reconstruction' of political rituals in the age of Louis XIV. It is therefore necessary to place these micro-events in a wider context.

When he succeeded to the throne in 1643, the child-king Louis inherited a rich symbolic capital of rituals. The major reference book for royal rituals in France, Denys Godefroy's huge *Cérémonial François* (1619, second edition 1649), confined itself to three main kinds of event, coronations, marriages and funerals, but we may

---

[13] Cf. Thomas Schelling, *The Strategy of Conflict* (Cambridge, Mass., 1960), 128.
[14] Menestrier (1691), 51.

also include the royal touch and the *lit de justice*.¹⁵ The *lits de justice* were gradually abandoned, leaving a space which needed to be filled. It was filled, and in an extremely creative manner. It is a pity that we do not know and probably shall never know who invented the new traditions – the king himself, his ministers, or his masters of ceremonies.¹⁶

Before the king came to reside more or less permanently in the 'palace of the sun', he used it as the setting for *fêtes*..¹⁷ As is well known, three of these events were of particular importance, politically and culturally. The first, in 1664, was a romantic, chivalric festival organized around the theme of 'Les Plaisirs de l'Île Enchantée', allowing the king and his courtiers to play the roles of Roger (Ariosto's Ruggiero), of Roland, Oliver, Ogier the Dane, and other paladins. The second, in 1668, was more political, and celebrated the successful conclusion of the War of Devolution.

The third festival, and grandest of all, took place in 1674, following the return of Louis 'the Great' (as he was now styled officially) from the Dutch war, and represented his achievements both literally (the crossing of the Rhine) and allegorically (via Hercules and Minerva). These spectacles or performances were on the margin of ritual in the strict sense of the term, but they illustrate very well the different links between politics and culture. They impressed viewers with the king's 'magnificence', they presented Louis as a hero, and in addition the second and third festivals offered interpretations of recent political events.

Splendid as they were, these three fêtes followed a tradition which had been established by the Renaissance, if not before.¹⁸ There was more innovation in another ritual domain, that of the everyday life of the king. This everyday life had long been ritualized, but changes in the ritual can be discerned over the long

---

[15] Sarah Hanley, *The Lit de Justice of the Kings of France* (Princeton, 1983); Richard Jackson, *Vive le roi!* (Chapel Hill, 1984); Ralph Giesey, `Models of Rulership in French Royal Ceremonial', in *Rites of Power*, ed. Sean Wilentz (Philadelphia, 1985), 41-64; see also the chapter by Michèle Fogel, in the volume *Le Protocole*, ed. Deloye, 1996.

[16] Some of these inventions are discussed in Gérard Sabatier's contribution to the volume *Le Protocole*, ed. Deloye, 1996.

[17] Marie-Christine Moine, *Les fêtes à la cour du roi soleil* (Paris, 1984).

[18] Jean Jacquot (ed), *Les Fêtes de la Renaissance* (3 vols, Paris 1956-75).

term. As Saint-Simon pointed out with regret, there is always the danger that 'une nouveauté faite par une ignorance' might 'tourner en usage et en règle'.[19] Again, the move to Versailles necessarily altered traditional rituals in important respects. As the popes discovered when they migrated to Avignon, rituals cannot be moved from one locale to another without undergoing transformations.

In the case of the rituals of Louis XIV, there is also evidence of deliberate reconstruction. For example, there was an attempt to make Versailles a special place, almost a sacred place.

The fullest evidence comes from a famous courtesy-book, Courtin's *Nouveau traité de la civilité*, which tells its readers how to behave when they visit the palace, which was open to everyone of respectable appearance. Visitors were instructed not to envelop themselves in their cloaks (presumably because they might be concealing daggers); not to knock on doors but simply to scratch them; not to lean on the arm of the king's empty chair; and to remove their hats even in the antechambers, and especially in the empty room where the table is laid for the royal meal. On entering the king's empty bedroom, men should remain uncovered, while ladies should make an act of reverence to the royal bed.[20] These rituals might be regarded as archaic survivals from the age of the priest-kings; but the sacralization of the secular might also be viewed as an ironic consequence of the gradual secularization of post-medieval culture.

Versailles itself was reconstructed physically in part to serve as a more appropriate setting for the reconstructed rituals. The royal *lever* and *coucher* were not new customs, but they received more emphasis in their new setting. Again, the formal visits by ambassadors on arrival (the presentation of credentials) and departure (the *congé*), were established diplomatic rituals, but they became more impressive and dramatic once l'Escalier des Ambassadeurs came into use. Ambassadors from distant lands (among them the Ottoman Empire, Persia, and Siam), might see

---

[19] Louis duc de Saint-Simon, *Mémoires*, ed. Yves Coirault (8 vols, Paris 1983-8), vol. 1, 449.
[20] Antoine Courtin, *Nouveau traité de la civilité* (Paris, 1671).

the king sitting on a silver throne, a piece of ritual equipment which seems to have been considered too archaic for use on other occasions, but was believed to correspond to the expectations of 'orientals'. As was traditional, the ritualized exchange of gifts was central to these formal encounters.

The palace served as a setting for more modern rituals. Following his move to Versailles in 1682, Louis instituted his *appartements*. In other words he opened some of his rooms to the nobility three times a week for billiards, cards, conversation and refreshments. These occasions deserve to be described as 'rituals' (even if they were less ritualized and more spontaneous than, say, the royal touch), because they were devised in order to display the king's accessibility to his subjects, a point emphasized in the official media of the time (from medals to the *Mercure Galant*). In practice, according to Saint-Simon, Louis soon failed to make an appearance, but the theatre of accessibility continued to run for a long time thereafter.[21]

Outside Versailles, there were other new rituals. The unveiling of statues to the king, for example, with what Saint-Simon described with some malice as 'cérémonies tirées et imitées de la consécration de celles des empereurs romains'[22] From the point of view of 'sécularisation', these ceremonies deserve an extended analysis.[23]

An important complex of new rituals were those associated with international peace congresses, notably Münster (1648), Nijmegen (1678) Rijswijck (1697), and Utrecht (1712). Apart from the work of Lucien Bély on Utrecht, the congresses have not been studied from this point of view. Visits and dinners as well as formal sessions of negotiation may be viewed as so many rituals, with rules to follow (or occasionally to transgress) in order to communicate symbolic messages.[24]

The question of precedence remained a difficult one, as was necessarily the case in societies which were both hierarchical and

---

[21] Saint-Simon, vol. 1, 36.
[22] Saint-Simon, vol. 1, 630.
[23] Cf Sabatier in the volume *Le Protocole*, ed. Deloye, 1996.
[24] Lucien Bely, *Espions et ambassadeurs au temps de Louis XIV* (Paris, 1990), 377, 394, and especially 411ff.

mobile. Disputes over coaches continued to occur, as in the case of the Marquis de Torcy and the Venetian ambassador.[25] Again, at Utrecht, the insults exchanged between the servants of the French ambassador and those of a deputy from Overijssel when his coach passed in front of the ambassador's house became a *cause célèbre*.[26]

It was to avoid some of the recurrent and awkward problems of precedence that circular or oval tables came into use (whether consciously or unconsciously, following the precedent of the court of King Arthur). As Saint-Simon remarked on the congress of Rijswijck, negotiations took place 'autour d'une table ronde pour éviter toute dispute de rang'.[27] Or as the contemporary description of the rules to be followed at Utrecht put it, 'les portes, la table et les chaises sont disposés de manière qu'il n'y a ni haut ni bas bout, et par conséquent nulle distinction. On a fait de concert le règlement sur le modèle de celui de Ryswick'.[28]

3. The formation of protocol

In this section I shall try to situate the official attitude to political ritual in the age of Louis XIV in the perspective of *la longue durée*.

In the first place, I should like to suggest that this period was decisive for the crystallization of the new forms of what Erving Goffman calls 'interaction ritual', forms which have lasted till our own time in the world of diplomacy.[29] Permanent ambassadors were of course an invention of the Italian Renaissance.[30] The audiences of these ambassadors to the rulers to whom they were accredited were of course ritualized occasions. However, a special cluster of diplomatic rituals had not yet developed.

The conventional wisdom declares that diplomatic protocol dates from the Congress of Vienna in 1815, an occasion in which

---
[25] Bely (1990), 689.
[26] Bely (1990), 406ff.
[27] Saint-Simon, vol. 1, 389.
[28] Quoted Bely (1990), 412.
[29] Erving Goffman, *Interaction Ritual* (New York, 1967).
[30] Garrett Mattingly, *Renaissance Diplomacy* (London, 1956).

considerable attention was devoted to the subject. The Congress is certainly cited as an important precedent in later manuals of diplomacy, such as those of Charles Martens, Ernest Satow, or, to bring the story more or less up to date, the handbook to protocol by John Wood and Jean Serres.[31]

However, a comparison of this latter handbook with two famous texts from the age of Louis XIV will serve to show the extent to which 'modern' protocol was a creation of the late seventeenth and early eighteenth centuries, the age of the famous congresses of Rijswijck and Utrecht. The first text was the work of a Dutchman, Abraham de Wicquefort (1598-1682), a diplomat in the service of the rulers of Brandenburg and Brunswick, while the second came from the pen of a former secretary to Louis XIV, François de Callières. The subject of both books is the function of the ambassador and the art of negotiation. Both books offer detailed descriptions of the rules for audiences, visits, and precedence. In the course of their discussion, they do not fail to refer to the London brawl. Wicquefort declares at one point that the coach of an ambassador should be 'inviolable'.[32]

The emphasis on ritual and its political efficacy by these authors deserves comment. As Wicquefort put it, 'les civilités et les cérémonies' are among the 'parties les plus essentielles de l'Ambassade', so that 'un grand exterieur, et une belle apparence' offer the ambassador 'de plus notables avantages que ... la vertu même'.[33] Both these authors compare the ambassador to an actor. 'Pour réussir en cette profession il faut estre un peu comedien'. 'Un Ambassadeur ressemble en quelque manière à un comédien, exposé sur le théâtre aux yeux du public pour y jouer de grands rôles'.[34] It is time to turn to the idea of political theatre in general.

---

[31] Anon, Règlement (1815); Charles de Martens, *Le guide diplomatique* (2 vols, Leipzig, 1832); Ernest Satow, *A Guide to Diplomatic Practice* (London, 1917); Jules Cambon, *Le diplomate* (Paris, 1926); John R. Wood and Jean Serres, *Diplomatic Ceremonial and Protocol* (London, 1970).
[32] Abraham Wicquefort, *L'ambassadeur* (2 vols, The Hague 1680-1), 721ff, 896; Callières (1716), 91. Cf. *Règlement* (1713), q. Bély (1990) 413.
[33] Wicquefort (1680-1), 416, 10-11.
[34] Wicquefort (1680-1), 10; Callières (1716), 18.

4. Three Styles of Political Theatre

In a broad sense of the term 'theatre', all politics has a theatrical aspect in the sense that attempts to persuade involve a dramatization of the issues at stake, a dramatization which frequently turns into the re-enactment of certain basic stories, metaphors or myths, such as the victory of good over evil, order over chaos, and purity over corruption. Louis XIV was frequently presented as a hero destroying a monster (representing various incarnations of evil and disorder, such as the Fronde, Calvinism or the Triple Alliance between England, Holland and the Empire).

In the middle of the twentieth century, in electoral campaigns different parts of the Americas, more than one candidate (Jânio Quadros in Brazil, for instance) appeared with a broom, symbolizing his determination to sweep away the debris of the previous regime.[35]

All the same, styles of political drama, like those of theatre in the literal sense, vary from place to place and from period to period. There are changes in dramatic conventions, in the composition of the audiences, and possibly in the function of the plays.

I shall present these final reflections in the form of a triangular comparison, discussing a study of nineteenth-century Bali and a study of the contemporary west from the viewpoint of a historian of the sixteenth and seventeenth centuries.

1. The first thesis on which I should like to comment here is central to the famous study by Clifford Geertz on what he calls the 'theater state' of nineteenth-century Bali. This was a state in which, according to the author, it is mistaken to assume, like many western political scientists, that ritual is a medium in the service of power. For the Balinese, as Geertz presents them, the reverse was the case. The Balinese state was weak but spectacular. Its very *raison d'être* was spectacle.

I will not presume to comment on the reliability of Geertz's account of Bali (though it is worth mentioning that his central

---
[35] Murray Edelman, *Politics as Symbolic Action* (Chicago, 1971); Kertzer (1988).

thesis has been criticized by other specialists on South-East Asia).[36] The question I should like to ask is whether seventeenth-century France was a 'theatre state' in the Geertzian sense of the term. It is indeed tempting to use this phrase, given the millions of *livres* poured into the construction of Versailles, the daily spectacles in which the king played the principal role, and in which the leading nobles, *les grands*, were obliged to participate.

On the other hand, the rituals or the theatre of politics were viewed in a more instrumental way than they were in Bali as Geertz presents it. The young Louis may have enjoyed spectacle for its own sake, but the middle-aged Colbert, for instance, expected a political return from every *livre* spent on display.

In any case, France was a relatively strong state Louis XIV had a large army and used it to enforce his will at home and abroad. He did not rely on ritual alone to establish his position as the leading European monarch. Ritual was a weapon rather than a 'barometer', but it was not the only weapon in the royal arsenal.

2. In the 1970s, a study of modern politics by Roger-Gérard Schwartzenberg suggested that the age of television was also that of the rise of *L'Etat-spectacle*.[37] It is obvious that contemporary politics can be viewed as a spectacle, and it is certainly plausible to argue that the rise of television has had important political consequences. For example, it makes politicians conscious of the cameras (as in the notorious case of Senator Joe McCarthy) and encourages them to play their role in new ways.[38]

All the same, the Schwartzenberg thesis ignores the importance of earlier political spectacles, as the author himself seems to have realized when he made a brief reference to Louis XIV in a paragraph which appears inconsistent with the main argument of his study.[39] As Queen Elizabeth I once expressed it, in her so-

---

[36] Stanley J. Tambiah, `A Reformulation of Geertz' Conception of the Theatre State', in his *Culture, Thought and Social Action* (Cambridge MA, 1985, 316-38).
[37] Roger-Gérard Schwartzenberg, *L'Etat-spectacle: essai sur et contre le star system en politique* (Paris, 1977).
[38] Richard H. Rovere, *Senator Joe McCarthy* (London, 1960).
[39] Schwartzenberg, 263.

called 'Tilbury speech', 'We princes I tell you are set on stages'.
The example of Louis XIV is only one of many which could be quoted from the early modern period to show that rulers were already conscious performers. An Italian who visited Versailles in the 1670s noted how Louis behaved differently in public and in private. In his *cabinet*, he abandons gravity, but if the door opens, 'il se compose aussitôt son attitude et prend une autre expression de figure, comme s'il devait paraître sur un théâtre' (see below, ch. 9).[40]

Some of the problems of 'managing' the appearance of rulers on-stage remain constant over the centuries. For instance, Louis XIV was only one in a series of leading men and women (Charles I, Napoleon, Ceauşescu, Elizabeth II, etc) whose actual height did not match their social height, and had to be disguised in some way or other.

However, it is more fruitful to analyse changes over the centuries. How did Louis' style of theatre differ from the political theatre of today?[41] At this point the repercussions on ritual of 'les revendications égalitaires et démocratiques' become obvious.

For one thing, the audience which the king and the government had in mind was not the people, 'les vingt millions de Français', as Pierre Goubert has called them, but a narrower group or groups. In the first place, foreign monarchs. In the second place, domestic elites. In the third place, posterity.

Linked to the contrast between seventeenth-century and contemporary spectators are important differences in the style of spectacle. Louis had to be presented in a dignified manner. The smile on the face of the king's equestrian statue by Bernini was enough to ensure its rejection. Louis liked to think of himself as accessible, unlike his Spanish rival, but by twentieth-century standards he was symbolically distanced from the public.

Such distanciation of the leader would be a form of political suicide in many countries today. What is required today is the

---

[40] Primi Visconti, *Mémoires sur la cour de Louis XIV*, ed. Jean-François Solnon (Paris, 1988), 28.
[41] Cf Peter Burke, *The Fabrication of Louis XIV* (New Haven, 1992: French translation, *Louis XIV; les stratégies de la gloire*, Paris 1994), ch. 12.

illusion of intimacy, created by the shaking of hands, kissing of babies, and so on. Equally important is the illusion of energy, youth and vitality. Despite his age, George Bush Senior was frequently to be seen jogging – in front of the television cameras. Louis XIV posed for his portraits in armour or in his coronation robes. He dressed up to be painted. Contemporary heads of state on the other hand often dress down, removing ties and even shirts for television interviews (as former president Collor of Brazil did on occasion), in order to seem closer to the people. Putin's barebreasted image has its place in a tradition.

In short, I am sceptical about the idea of 'la théâtralisation de la politique' if this phrase is to be understood as a process of increasing theatricality over the centuries. It would surely be better to speak of differences in style. The development of protocol was not the invention of a new drama, but the formalization of the conventions for a political theatre which had already had a very long run.

9: ON THE MARGINS OF THE PUBLIC AND THE PRIVATE: LOUISE XIV AT VERSAILLES

In 1673 a young Italian nobleman, Primi Visconti, arrived in Paris and as one might have expected he visited the court of Louis XIV. He observed the king's behaviour on a number of occasions, and when he later wrote his memoirs, he had this to say about Louis, who was in his mid-thirties at the time of observation (Visconti, 1988, 28).[1]

> In public, he is full of gravity and very different from his manner in private [*particolare*]. Finding myself in his chamber together with other courtiers, I have observed on a number of occasions that if the door is accidentally opened, or if he goes out, he immediately composes his posture and changes his facial expression, as if he was going to appear on stage.

We might speak of Louis as crossing not only a literal threshold but also a frontier of identity, caught by Visconti at the moment of switching between his public and private selves, a process something like the code-switching studied by sociolinguists.

---

[1] Written in Italian, this text was first published in French by Jean Lemoine in 1908. It was first published in Italian in 1945, but translated from the French. My thanks to Francesco Boldizzoni for clearing up this problem.

Jumping over a gap of nearly three centuries, it may be instructive to compare this description of the king with one of Senator Joseph McCarthy who, so we learn from a reporter who observed him at first hand, 'was capable of going into a tantrum before the television cameras' and then walking away to 'a corner of the room outside the sweep of the television cameras, there to observe calmly and be amused by the commotion he had caused', moving from normal to paranoid and back in moments (Rovere 1959, 54-5, 58). Conversely, it is worth noting the occasions when political actors believe that the microphone is switched off, as in the case of George W. Bush talking to Tony Blair at a Group of Eight meeting in St Petersburg in 2006, believing, falsely as it turned out, that he had already crossed the frontier into the private sphere (Reported by the BBC 17 July 2006, *news.bbc.co.uk*).

I believe in the potential of an anthropological approach to politics, including fieldwork in parliaments and if possible in committees and corridors of power. This is an approach that should surely include a historical anthropology. The idea of an anthropologist at the court of Louis XIV may seem almost as odd as that of a Yankee at the court of King Arthur. All the same, there is not infrequently a close fit between anthropological observations and observations made in the seventeenth century itself, not only by foreigners but by natives as well.

The writer Jean La Bruyère, for instance, observed (1688, 213) that in a country 'more than eleven hundred leagues by sea from the Iroquois and the Hurons', there was a chapel (meaning the chapel of Versailles) where 'the people seem to adore their prince, and their prince appears to worship God'. Again, in his study of the court system, the French historian Emmanuel Le Roy Ladurie presented the Duc de Saint-Simon as a kind of anthropologist *avant la lettre*, comparing his interest in hierarchy to that of Louis Dumont.

Within this anthropological approach, there seems a place for the study of borders. Returning to the passage of Visconti's memoirs, quoted above: if it had not been the subject of comment by earlier historians of Louis XIV but impressed me when I first came across it, this was probably because I had already read Erving Goffman (1959), a sociologist who behaved like an anthropologist.

I

In his famous essay on *The Presentation of Self in Everyday Life*, Goffman (1959) distinguishes between what he calls 'front regions', where performances take place, and 'back regions'. To illustrate the distinction he quotes (121-2) a marvellous passage from George Orwell, writing – in 1933 – about waiters.

> It is an instructive sight to see a waiter going into a hotel dining-room. As he passes the door a sudden change comes over him. The set of his shoulders alters; all the dirt and hurry and irritation have dropped off in an instant. He glides over the carpet with a solemn priest-like air.

That is one kind of frontier: a line that is crossed in an instant. Another kind, more like a zone that takes some time to traverse, is discussed by Victor Turner in his famous studies of rites of passage such as initiations and of liminality in general.

As one commentator has remarked, in 1969, with his *Ritual Process*, Turner himself 'crossed the threshold' from a more precise to a broader use of the concept (Babcock, 2001). He was sometimes criticized for making everything seem liminal, and in response he came to distinguish (1974, 640) between the narrower term 'liminal' and the wider 'liminoid', resembling the liminal but not identical with it.

It is possible to view Louis XIV from Turner's perspective. The king was no stranger to rites of passage. His baptism had turned him into a Christian, his coronation or *sacre* into a king and his marriage into a husband, while his funeral explored the liminal region between life and death and between the king's reign and that of his successor (Burke, 1992). Turner also argued (1974) that we learn from disorder, that an 'anti-structure', as he called it, may be regarded as the precursor of a new structure, and in this case it is worth noting that Louis learned from his unhappy experience of the Fronde, the mainly aristocratic rebellion that took place in his youth, when a crowd invaded the Louvre, and that this memory of disorder underlay his efforts to create what historians describe as his 'absolute monarchy'.

All the same, it is not Turner or the rites of passage that interested him so much that will be discussed here. In what follows the emphasis will fall not on the making or cultural construction of the king but on his reconstruction, in other words the maintenance of his position through everyday performances, the daily metamorphosis of a rather small man into 'Louis le Grand' (his official title) thanks to rituals and other props to identity such as clothes – as the novelist William Thackeray brilliantly demonstrated in a satirical drawing (*https://commons.wikimedia.org/.../File:1840_engraving_depicting_Louis_XIV_of_Fr...*). The following anthropological view of Versailles will view the palace through Goffman's spectacles. Its focus will be on relatively rapid passages from one royal role, identity or style of performance to another.

II

It is important to avoid identifying formality with the artificial and informality with the real or the sincere. Louis talking to a few select courtiers before going through the door was also in a sense performing, following not a script but the promptings of the royal habitus that he had learned very early in life (he became king when he was five years old, following his father's death in 1643). All the same, there were differences between his formal and informal styles of performance, even if we know all too little about the informal style. For example, did the king take off his wig in his cabinet? In front of the courtiers? In front of Madame de Maintenon? We do not know.

The problem of the frontier between performance and reality was a general preoccupation in the seventeenth century, at least among the upper classes. The language commonly used to discuss the problem was the contrast between *être* and *paraître*, *Sein* and *Schein*, *ser* and *parecer*, and the need for unmasking, what the Spaniards called *desengaño*. One might link this preoccupation, or at least the language used to discuss it, to the rise of theatres and scenery and their consequent 'reality effects'. It may be instructive to make comparisons with our own time, with the rise of virtual reality and of performance art, 'liminal acts' that cross the threshold between performance and audience (Broadhurst 1999).

Plays within plays were not uncommon in the age of the baroque (Forestier 1981): among them were the *Comédie des comédiens* (1631) of Gougenot, the play of the same title by Georges de Scudéry (1634) and *L'illusion comique* (1635) by Pierre Corneille. The legend of St Genesius had considerable appeal at this time. According to the legend, Genesius was an actor at the time of the emperor Diocletian, who was converted to Christianity in the act of playing a Christian martyr and then martyred himself. The story inspired the Spanish dramatist Lope de Vega Carpio's *Fingido verdadero* (1620), *L'illustre comédien* (1644) by Nicolas Desfontaines and, most famously, *St Genest* (c.1645) by Jean Rotrou (Buffum 1957, 212-39).

These plays illustrate another major baroque theme, metamorphosis (Rousset 1953). The concern with change raises the problem of liminality once again: in the famous sculpture by Bernini, illustrating Ovid's *Metamorphoses*: where does Daphne end and the laurel tree begin?

This discussion of theatre may seem a digression from politics, but it is not. 'We princes I tell you are set as it were upon stages in the sight and view of the world', Queen Elizabeth is supposed to have remarked in the age of Shakespeare and *The Globe* (Levin 2003). The court may be seen as a stage, the scene of the dramatization or ritualization of the everyday activities of the ruler, notably his *lever* and *coucher* at the thresholds of night and day (Gunn and Janse 2006, 2).

Contemporaries were well aware of the theatrical aspect of courts. The language of Visconti, already quoted, or that of the famous memoirs of the Duc de Saint-Simon, who often used the words *scène*, for instance (vol.1, 714, 857; vol. 3, 86, 92, 105, 109), when writing about Versailles. He also refers to *comédie*, or *theatre* (vol.1, 781, 811; vol.3, 233, 579, 733, 774, 957).

To illustrate the theatre of the court one might take the example of the so-called *appartements*. Following his permanent move to Versailles in 1682, Louis opened some of the more private rooms in the palace to his courtiers three times a week for them to play billiards or cards, engage in conversation and take refreshments. It is stretching the term a little, but not too much, to describe these semi-formal occasions as 'rituals', or at the very least as ritualized, since they were devised to communicate a message, to display the king's accessibility to his subjects. In practice, Louis soon failed to make an appearance on these occasions, but the theatre of accessibility continued to run for a long time.

Within the theatre of the court as in other theatres the distinction between front and back, on stage and off-stage, was an important one. The English already spoke at this time of what went on 'behind the scenes' (Addison, himself a playwright, did so in 1711), while Saint-Simon (vol.3, 88, 312, 458, etc) wrote about *les derrières*. What Italian students of politics call *dietrologia* is not so new after all.

Palace architecture both reflected and encouraged this distinction between front and back. As we have seen, Visconti already mentioned the royal *chambre* in the period before the king moved into Versailles. After he did so the old public rooms were converted into private rooms for the king, called *cabinets*, into which a few favoured courtiers were admitted (Saint-Simon was not included). These rooms included the *cabinet des médailles* and the *cabinet du conseil* (though they were used for other purposes as well), while the old *antichambre* became a room for Louis to play billiards and feed his dogs (Newton 2000, 125).

The rooms were not exactly private – the binary opposition between public and private is not a useful one in this context. In any case, essentializing is particularly inappropriate when dealing with liminality. At the Versailles of Louis XIV, it is more illuminating to work with the idea of degrees of privacy and a

On the Margins of the Public and the Private: Louis XIV at Versailles

liminal zone or zones of transition. There appears to have been not one 'back region' but a succession of regions, a kind of *enfilade*.

There were major changes in the spatial arrangements during the king's long reign – more than half a century of effective rule. They become apparent if one compares the first Versailles (a hunting lodge used by the king's father, Louis XIII) with the *château* of Marly, a relatively small palace near Versailles where the king began to spend his leisure hours, together with select courtiers, in the later 1680s. Both palaces were originally constructed to allow the ruler to escape at least some of the everyday formality of the court, and both of them gradually became formalized in their turn.

There were other frontiers between public and private in the milieu of Louis XIV, even if they were less sharp than they would be in later centuries – or less visible, or drawn in different places than they would be later. Frontiers between what was known and what might be said, for instance, or between what was written and what might be printed. Two famous anecdotes cast a little light on these thresholds. Whether the stories were true or not, they were certainly current in the period and so they have something to tell us about seventeenth-century attitudes.

The first story concerns the courtier Roger de Rabutin, Comte de Bussy and his *Histoire Amoureuse* des Gaules, an allegorical novel written in 1665 about sexual intrigues at court, including those of the king himself. Louis enjoyed reading something that Bussy had written and as long as the 'amorous history' circulated (in manuscript) among the right people, the author experienced no problems. When it began to circulate more widely (and even printed, in 1665), however, the king was offended and Bussy was imprisoned in the Bastille (Duchêne 1992, 155, 163-7, 175-85).

The second anecdote, told by Saint-Simon (vol.1, 610), concerns a gaffe committed by the playwright Jean Racine, who was at one time in sufficient favour to be invited into the more private rooms of Versailles because Louis enjoyed his conversation. One day Racine accidentally referred to the writer Paul Scarron, in the presence of the king. The problem was that Scarron was the first husband of Madame de Maintenon, while her second husband was the king himself. The marriage was a secret one but it was known abroad, in England for instance. It must have been known at home as well, but the topic was taboo. Everyone knew, but the king should never know that they knew.

For us, observing early modern courts from our position in the twenty-first century, the frontier between public and private is often difficult to discern. It was a vague zone rather than a precise line. Officials often treated state papers as their private property, for instance, and left them to their heirs. Rulers gave audience to ministers or supplicants, received information and took decisions while they were hunting, being shaved, or even relieving themselves.

From the late fifteenth to the late seventeenth century, for instance, the Privy –in other words, private – Chamber formed a central part of the court. The Privy Chamber was a group of about fifteen people headed by the 'Groom of the Stool', who attended the king everywhere. The Groom was in charge of the maintenance and transport of the royal close-stools, hence his title, but they gave him a position of power, since he was able to control access to the king, to allow or forbid individuals to catch the royal eye or whisper in the royal ear. The groom was a liminal person, a gatekeeper (Starkey 1977).

Following this tradition, Louis XIV gave private audiences while sitting on his portable *chaise percée* (Newton 2006, 75). Even the king's sex life was semi-public. Although there appears to be no evidence in the archives concerning this part of his life, every time Louis made love to one of his mistresses there must have been at least two observers present, a valet and also a bodyguard, one of the *huissiers de la chambre* who guarded the entrance to the room where the king happened to be (Newton 2006, 68). One might describe these servants as liminal people in the sense that they were both there and not there at the same time.

Again, at the time of his operation for the fistula, Louis' private parts were the subject of public commentary in a way that one might have thought inconceivable today – or at least, until the

Clinton-Lewinsky affair. This relatively recent example prompts a final question: whether, thanks to intrusive media, such as photojournalism and especially television, the world is returning to the seventeenth-century situation. In principle, what many citizens want is transparency in government. In practice, they are offered another kind of transparency: what the butler saw, a view through the keyhole of the presidential bedroom.

References

Babcock, B. A. (2001) 'Liminality.' In: Smelser, N. J. and Baltes, P. J. (eds.) *International Encyclopedia of the Social & Behavioral Sciences*. 26 vols., Amsterdam and Oxford: Elsevier, vol. 13, 8862-4.

Broadhurst, S. (1999) *Liminal Acts: a critical overview of contemporary performance theory*. London: Cassell.

Buffum, I. (1957) *Studies in the Baroque from Montaigne to Rotrou*. New Haven: Yale University Press.

Burke, P. (1992) *The Fabrication of Louis XIV*. New Haven: Yale University Press.

Donnan, H. 'Borders, anthropology of.' In: Smelser, N. J. and Baltes, P. J. (eds.) *International Encyclopedia of the Social & Behavioral Sciences*. 26 vols., Amsterdam and Oxford: Elsevier, vol.2, 1290-3.

Duchêne, J. (1992) *Bussy-Rabutin*. Paris: Fayard.

Forestier, G. (1981) *Le Théâtre dans le théâtre sur la scène française du XVIIe siècle*. Geneva: Droz.

Goffman, E. (1959) *The Presentation of Self in Everyday Life*. New York: Doubleday.

Gunn. S. and Janse, A. (eds., 2006) *The Court as a Stage*. Leiden: Brill.

Jouhaud, C. (2007) *Sauver le Grand-Siècle?* Paris: Seuil.

La Bruyère, J. (1688) *Les Caractères ou les Mœurs de ce siècle.* Translated by Henry Van Laun, London: Nimmo.

Le Roy Ladurie, E. (1997) *Saint-Simon ou le système de la cour.* Paris: Fayard.

Levin, C. (2003) '"We Princes, I tell you, are set on stages": Elizabeth I and Dramatic Self- Representation.' in Cerasano, S. and Wynne-Davies, M. (eds.) *Readings in Renaissance Women's Drama.* London: Taylor and Francis.

Newton, W. R. (2000) *L'espace du roi: la cour de France au château de Versailles, 1682-1789.* Paris: Fayard.

Newton, W. R. (2006) *La petite cour: services et serviteurs à la cour de Versailles au 18e siècle.* Paris: Fayard.

Rousset, J. (1953) *La littérature de l'âge baroque en France: Circé et le Paon.* Paris: Conti.

Rovere, R. H. (1959) *Senator Joe McCarthy.* Rpr Berkeley: University of California Press, 1996.

Saint-Simon, Duc de (1983-88) *Mémoires.* Ed. Y. Coirault, 8 vols., Paris: Gallimard

Starkey D. (1977) 'Representation through Intimacy', in Lewis, I. M. (ed.) *Symbols and Sentiments: cross-cultural studies in symbolism.* New York: Academic Press.

Turner, V. W. (1964) 'Betwixt and Between: the liminal period in *rites de passage.*' In: Turner, *The Forest of Symbols: aspects of Ndembu Ritual.* Ithaca and London: Cornell University Press, 93-111.

Turner, V. W. (1969) *The Ritual Process: structure and anti-structure.* London: Routledge.

Turner, V. W. (1974) 'Liminal to Liminoid in play, flow and ritual: an essay in comparative symbolology.' In: *Rice University Studies* 60, 53-92.

Vinha, M. Da (2004) *Les valets de chambre de Louis XIV.* Paris: Perrin.

Visconti, P. (1988) *Mémoires sur la cour de Louis XIV, 1673-1681.* Ed. Solnon, J.-F. Paris: Perrin.

10: Representing Women's Work in Early Modern Italy

Tronca il filo, ed è il fil di viver mio:
Martella i fogli, ed il mio cor martella:
Legagli, e son tra lor legata anch'io.

[She cuts the thread, and it is the thread of my life:
She hammers the leaves, and it is my heart that she is hammering:
She binds them, and I too am bound among them.]

These lines describing a female bookbinder at work come from a poem entitled 'Bella Libraia', by Gianfrancesco Maia Materdona.[1] In seventeenth-century Italy, there was a fashion for poems describing women at work. Why should this have been the case? It was the attempt to solve the puzzle that led to the writing of this paper. It turned out that in order to replace the poems in their cultural context, it would be necessary to study other representations of women's work.

It has become a commonplace that early modern women – like women in other pre-industrial societies – were long invisible to historians, not only because most of them were males who did not take sufficient interest in the doings of the opposite sex, but also because women did not occur very frequently in the sources

---
[1] Benedetto Croce (ed.) *Lirici marinisti* (Bari, 1910), 111.

(themselves also created for the most part by men).² In the case of women's work, the fact that women were generally excluded from the guilds (despite the exceptions made for widows of former members or in the case of particular guilds such as sellers of bouquets and *lingerie* in Paris) gave the misleading impression that most females did not work.

In the last generation, however, the rise of interest in women's history on one side, and in the history of the informal economy on the other, has allowed a picture of women's work to be reconstructed from a variety of sources including the judicial archives, in which records of disputes reveal women selling from stalls or from house to house.³ In the case of early modern Italy, a vivid image of working women may be obtained by comparing or triangulating three rather different sources. One of these is obvious, the census. A second, long neglected by historians in general, but increasingly exploited in the last twenty years or so, is the evidence of images, whether paintings or prints. The third source to be discussed in this chapter is the one with which it began: poetry. The rise of a poetic genre describing women at work becomes more intelligible if it is placed in the context of other representations of labour in this period.

In the pages that follow these three sources will be discussed not as a means to reconstruct the world of working women but as evidence of increasing interest in different forms of work on the part of contemporaries, especially men from the upper classes. My hypothesis is that the production of different kinds of representation of work in this period was the response to a rise in demand.

I

In the first place, then, the census, more exactly the censuses of one major city, Venice, regarded not as a transparent or objective source but rather as what Emile Durkheim called a 'collective

---
² Renate Bridenthal and Claudia Koonz (eds.) *Becoming Visible: Women in European History*, (Boston, 1977).
³ Merry E. Wiesner, *Women and Gender in Early Modern Europe* (Cambridge, 1993).

representation', a term all the more appropriate in this case because the census was carried out and recorded by a team.[4] Records of the census survive for five-sixths of the city in 1633, two-thirds (or four *sestieri*) in 1642 and one third in 1670. The parish priests were instructed to make a house to house survey of the inhabitants of their parish, presenting the results on printed forms which divided the population into nobles, citizens and 'artisans'. Since surnames were not yet common among the artisan class, the priests were instructed to write down the occupation of the head of each household. A substantial minority of household heads were women. Many are styled simply 'widow', but about 700 women were identified by occupation. Since there were over 60,000 women living in Venice in the middle of the seventeenth century, this sample is a small one, but the results may be of interest all the same.

The priests recorded 112 adjectives that referred to female occupations. This does not mean that 112 different occupations were available to women. The priests were not furnished with an official list of occupations but had to decide how to describe the job that the head of the household said that she was doing. Some wrote *allevatrice*, others *comare*, two terms that translate as 'midwife'. *Revedina*, *strazzaruola* and *venderigole* appear to be different terms describing the same occupation, a dealer in second-hand goods, especially clothes. It is a little more problematic to equate *fornera*, *pistora* and *panattariola*, in other words 'baker' or 'bread-seller', because there might have been some division of labour in this domain. In the case of the terms *cortegiana* and *meretrice*, it is likely that the terms stood respectively for the up-market and down-market versions of the same occupation.

It is this profession which most clearly reveals, like a litmus paper, the importance of the census as a representation. In Florence, where the census of 1631 was conducted by lay officials, 95 heads of household were described simply as *meretrici*. In

---

[4] Peter Burke, 'Classifying the People: The Census as Collective Representation', *Historical Anthropology of Early Modern Italy* (Cambridge, 1987), 27-39. The seventeenth-century censuses discussed here are in Venice, Archivio di Stato, Provveditori della Sanità, 568-72.

Venice, on the other hand, where it was the parish-priests who did the leg-work of collecting information, this occupation was not recorded in the same way as others. In the parish of San Marcilian, in 1642, for instance, 17 women were recorded as living alone. A large M is written against each name and it is explained that this means *meretrice*. The explanation suggests embarrassment or the desire to moralize, and reminds us that the collective representation was the work of different individuals with different attitudes. More details about women's work are given in some parishes than others, probably because certain priests were more interested in the topic than others (or indeed the government, for whom occupation was probably no more than a means of identification).

II

The census was made for practical reasons. For evidence of an increasing interest in working women we need to turn to the other two sources, images and poems. The value of visual evidence for the history of working women is obvious enough, given their relative invisibility in official documents, and some economic historians have made full use of it in studies of Mughal India and elsewhere.[5]

What concerns me here is a shift in the images of work (working women), from the background of paintings or prints (the Tower of Babel, for instance, or the months of the year)to their true subject-matter. This early modern shift was not confined to Italy. It is not difficult to find Spanish examples of paintings of this kind (including Velázquez, from the *Old Woman Cooking Eggs* to the more famous *Tapestry Weavers, Las Hilanderas*), French examples (including Jean-Baptiste Chardin and François Boucher), and above all Flemish and Dutch examples, including works by Pieter Aertsen, Jan Beuckelaer, Jacob Ochtervelt, Adrian van Ostade and Emmanuel de Witte.

---

[5] Ahsan Jan Qaisar, *Building Construction in Mughal India: the Evidence from Painting* (Delhi, 1988); a general discussion in Peter Burke, *Eyewitnessing* (London, 2001), 108-13.

From the early sixteenth century, and especially from the later seventeenth century onwards, a genre of print came into existence that represented street traders and was frequently known – paradoxically enough for a visual genre – as the 'Cries' of Paris, London and elsewhere. For example, Marcellus Laroon's *Cries of London* (1687) represented forty occupations (enlarged to seventy-four by 1689). The women represented include sellers of cherries, strawberries, oranges, wax or wafers, mackerel and fire shovels, and buyers of old satin and 'kitchen stuff', as well as a courtesan and a brothel Madam.[6]

There was also an Italian tradition of such images. Early examples include two early sixteenth-century drawings of domestic labour, Parmigianino's peasant woman kneading dough and Polidoro di Caravaggio's woman sewing. In the seventeenth and eighteenth centuries, these images become more frequent, they take the form of paintings and prints for the public to buy, and they extend to women's work outside the home.[7]

For some reason this tradition was particularly strong in Bologna, from the *Poultry market* by Bartolomeo Passarotti (1529-92) with women selling chickens and greengrocery, to the *Woman washing dishes* and the *Laundresses* by Giuseppe Maria Crespi (1665-1747) and the drawings of women embroidering and washing linen and the painting of women embroidering by Giuseppe Gambarini (1680-1725).[8]

Most famous of all were the drawings of different occupations, male and female, by Annibale Carracci (1560-1609), since they were made into prints after the death of the artist. Simon Guillain's engravings after Carracci, *Diverse figure* (1646) was followed by the prints of G. M. Mitelli, *Di Bologna l'arti* (1660), adapted from Carracci.[9] These series included a few women

---

[6] For Paris, Vincent Milliot, *Les cris de Paris ou le peuple travesti (16e-18e siècles): les représentations des petits métiers parisiens* (Paris, 1995); for London, Sean Shesgreen, *Images of the Outcast: The urban poor in the Cries of London* (Manchester, 2002), especially 45-7, on Laroon.
[7] On Italian prints, Karen F. Beall, *Cries and Itinerant Trades: a Bibliography* (Hamburg, 1975), 320-79.
[8] John T. Spike, *G. M. Crespi and the emergence of genre painting in Italy* (Fort Worth, 1986).
[9] Alessandro Marabottini, *Le arti di Bologna di Annibale Carracci* (Rome, 1979).

who sold articles in the streets: three in the *Diverse figure* and one in the Mitelli series.

Artists in other parts of Italy also participated in this genre. Vincenzo Campi (c1530-91) of Cremona painted *Fishwives* and *A Fruit Market*. Giacomo Ceruti (1698-1767), who came from Milan, made a number of paintings of women spinning and sewing, including *Ragazze che lavorono al tombolo* (in which five work and another girl reads to them).

Prints of trades based on local observation were also produced in Rome and Venice. Two hundred figures (all male) entitled *Quelli che vanno vendendo per Roma* were published in 1582 by Ambrosius Brambilla, followed by two hundred and forty figures by Nicolas van Aelst in 1600, including two women, one of whom sells hats.[10] The 1785 edition of *Le arti che vanno per le strade di Venezia* by Gaetano Zompini (1700-98) is composed of sixty etchings of Venetian street traders. Seven represent women in the act of selling milk, water, fried food and second-hand clothes as well as telling fortunes, hiring out servants and selling theatre and opera tickets.[11] By the early nineteenth century the fashion had spread to Milan and Naples and the number of working women represented had increased. Of the 30 trades represented in a Milan series from c1810, eight were female: poultry-seller, fruit-seller, flower-seller, linen-seller, herb-seller, fishwife, milliner and laundress. Of the 36 social types of Naples represented in a series of lithographs of 1829, seven were of working women, a laundress and sellers of sulphur water, maize, cod, eggs, chestnuts and tuna.[12]

It is time to return to the question of demand, posed earlier. For what kind of people were these images made? There is only a small amount of direct evidence, but what there is seems to be significant. Images of ordinary people working appealed to some members of the Italian upper classes. An early example is that of Francesco de' Medici, grand Duke of Florence, who commissioned for his study around 1570 a series of paintings of

---

[10] Maria Beatrice Sirolesi (ed.) *I venditori ambulanti di Roma* (Rome, 1994).
[11] Gaetano Zompini, *Le arti che vanno per le strade di Venezia* (Venice, 1785).
[12] Beall, *Bibliography*.

workshops including that of a goldsmith and others in which men are blowing glass and making woollen cloth. Francesco's scientific interests are well known, making him an appropriate patron for this kind of painting.[13] Other examples of aristocratic interest include Ferdinando de'Medici, who encouraged Crespi to make genre paintings; the Avogadro family, patrons of Ceruti; and count Anton Maria Zanetti, who encouraged Zompini to make his drawings and later etchings of street traders. In the case of Gambarini, a contemporary account notes that his 'little pictures of humble and low subjects' appealed to 'many noble families and citizens' as well as to foreigners.[14] The pattern was similar in France and England.[15]

It is also likely that the prints were made to appeal to foreign travellers at a time when travel for pleasure or 'tourism' was increasing. For example, the Carracci images were republished in Germany with German captions in 1738, and in Denmark, with Danish captions, in 1747. In similar fashion the 1711 edition of Laroon was captioned in French and Italian as well as English. The captions also tell us something about the way in which these prints were intended to be viewed. The series from Milan c1810 were labelled as costume prints. That the Naples series was intended to be viewed in the same way is suggested by the inclusion of ladies. It was the same story outside Italy. In 1799, for instance, 60 engravings of Chinese street traders were published in London under the title *The Costume of China*.[16]

As for representations of working women, it is likely that the interest taken in them by males was partly erotic. Pretty girls are not infrequently represented, as if they were marketing their charms as well as their wares. The 1711 edition of Laroon shows an image inscribed 'the merry milkmaid'. Zompini's images were relatively unusual in refusing to idealize the life of the poor and to show people rather than costumes.

---

[13] Luciano Berti, *Il principe del studiolo* (Florence, 1967).
[14] Zanotti quoted in Spike, *Crespi*, 173.
[15] Milliot, *Les cris*, 98-111; Shesgreen, *Images of the Outcast* 47-8.
[16] Beall, *Bibliography*, 26, 30.

III

This context of upper-class male interest in working women may help to solve the poetic puzzle with which this paper began. Unlike the images of working women, the poems to be discussed have evoked no interest, so far as I am aware, among social or cultural historians. All the same, at least sixteen Italian poets of the seventeenth century contributed to the genre, beginning with a major literary figure, Giambattista Marino (1569-1625).[17] Fifteen of these writers produced one or two poems on the subject (about twenty altogether). Marino began with 'a woman sewing'. His followers wrote poems about female servants, beggars and laundresses or women harvesting, telling fortunes, selling chickens, teaching girls, embroidering and spinning, as well as the book-binding described at the beginning of this article.

One poet, Agostino Agostini [or Augustini], published a volume of 128 sonnets describing as many female occupations, arranged in alphabetical order from *Acquavitara* to *Zingara*.[18] The list includes obvious female occupations such as *Balia* (wetnurse), *Cuoca* (cook), *Fruttarola* (fruit-seller), *Lavandaia* (laundress), *Locandara* (innkeeper), Maestra (schoolmistress), *Ortolana* (market gardener), and *Pescivendola* (fishwife). More or less plausibly, Agostini also includes *Barcaruola* (boatwoman), *Barbiera* (barber), *Librara* (bookbinder) *Netta Pozzi* (drain cleaner) and *Pittrice* (painter). Still more creative, at the expense of plausibility, he adds *Banchiera* (banker), *Chirurga* (surgeon), *Falegname* (carpenter) and *Ingegnera* (engineer), while the most surprising occupation on the list is probably *Conduttrice d'Elephante*.

---

[17] The names of the followers of Marino, in alphabetical order, are Claudio Achillini, Agostino Agostini, Giuseppe Battista, Lorenzo Casaburi, Scipione Errico, Girolamo Fontanella, Marcello Giovanetti, GianFrancesco Maia Materdona, Bernardo Morando, Pier Francesco Paoli, Ciro di Pers, Giuseppe Salamoni, Giovan Leone Sempronio, Ludovico Tingoli and Paolo Zazzaroni. The poems are most easily accessible in three anthologies: Benedetto Croce (ed.) *Lirici marinisti* (Bari, 1910); Giuseppe G. Ferrero (ed.) *Marino e i marinisti* (1954); Giovanni Getto (ed.) *Marino ed i Marinisti* (2 vols., Milan and Naples, 1962).
[18] Agostino Agostini, *Le belle faccendiere* (Ravenna, 1655).

What is the meaning and the context of this new genre? It might be better to speak of 'meanings' and contexts in the plural. In the first place, the literary context. Discontented with the High Renaissance style of Ariosto and Tasso, seventeenth-century poets were in pursuit of something new. They tried to show their wit or ingenuity (*ingenio, argutezza*) by disconcerting their readers. As Marino famously wrote, 'the aim of the poet is to surprise' (*E del poeta il fin la maraviglia*).[19] To this end they sought out the unusual, whether they were choosing metaphors or topics.

Paradoxically enough, the category of the unusual included everyday life, previously assumed to be unworthy of poetic notice. Thus the poets under discussion here wrote about everyday objects – in the life of elites, at least – such as hourglasses, clocks and arquebuses, and especially novelties such as tobacco. They described their mistresses when wearing spectacles or engaged in everyday activities such as combing their hair, reading, riding, swimming or dancing. The moral or erotic reflections that follow the description of each woman reveal the ingenuity of the poet.

The second point that I should like to make about these poems is that they appear to be *ekphrases*, descriptions of images. This classical literary genre was revived at the Renaissance. Marino's *Galleria* (1619), describing a collection of paintings in a gallery, is perhaps the most famous example of the genre in Italian literature. Marino also wrote an epitaph on the death of Annibale Carracci, whose drawings of street trades virtually launched the genre of urban 'cries'. Agostini's 128 sonnets not only demonstrated his ingenuity and creativity but also produce an equivalent effect as a series to the *Cries* of Bologna, Rome, Paris or London.

A third point concerns the intended or actual readership for these poems. It is worth noting that Agostini dedicated his poems to the Grand Duke of Tuscany, in other words to the family, the Medici, to which the patron of Crespi's pictures of working women also belonged.

---

[19] James V. Mirollo, *The Poet of the Marvelous* (New York, 1963).

IV

Juxtaposing the three sources discussed so far, it may be argued that the poems testify to an increasing interest in female labour on the part of certain upper-class Italian males. A few comments on the trend may be useful, distinguishing different kinds of gaze and placing the Italian evidence in comparative context. That the gaze was male and sometimes charged with eroticism can hardly be doubted. Poets stress the beauty of the working women they describe and some print-makers follow them in this respect.

We might also speak of the 'picturesque' gaze, noting that some images are presented as costume pieces, and that some, given their multilingual captions, were designed with an audience of tourists in mind. After all, the term 'picturesque' came into use in Britain, France and elsewhere in the context of the rise of travelling for pleasure by people acquainted with the work of landscape and genre painters and so prepared, if not conditioned, to see foreign countries in the same way.

However, these adjectives are not appropriate for the work of Crespi (say) or Zompini, or indeed the parish priests who recorded more details about women's work in the census than they had been asked. I am tempted to speak of the 'ethnographic' gaze, and to make comparisons with a few travellers, such as Montaigne or Philip Skippon in Italy or Lorenzo Magalotti in England and Sweden, who make acute observations on local customs.

If individuals such as Magalotti were exceptional, we might speak, like Lévi-Strauss, of a more general 'distant gaze' rather than a precisely ethnographic eye.[20] For example, in his *Caractères* (1688) the French moralist Jean La Bruyère offered a description of a peasant so distanciated as to present the man as scarcely human.[21] In his chapter on the court, he followed a similar strategy, speaking of the customs of a certain country, some thousands of miles from the land of the Iroquois.

---

[20] Claude Lévi-Strauss, *Le regard éloigné* (Paris, 1983).
[21] Discussed in Carlo Ginzburg, *Occhiacci di legno: nove riflessioni sulla distanza* (Milan, 1998), 25-30.

This gaze was extended to other continents. In 1799, for instance, a book was published in London under the title of *The Costume of China*, with sixty engravings of Chinese street traders. The book was based on a series of gouache paintings made by a Chinese artist, Puqua, for the western market. The series was followed in the 1830s by 360 ink drawings by Tinqua. Among the female occupations shown in these paintings and drawings are weaving, patching cloth, twisting silk, sewing shoes, drawing flowers and carrying pails of night-soil.[22]

It remains to attempt to explain the rise of the distant gaze. Travel within Europe and outside Europe was making people aware of the 'otherness' of other cultures. Urbanization was having similar effects at home. As cities grew in size, they became more diverse and the different social groups became more segregated from one another. In his chapter on the city, in other words, Paris, La Bruyère once again distanced himself from his subject and noted that 'La ville est partagée en diverses sociétés qui sont comme autant de petites républiques, qui ont leurs lois, leurs usages, leur jargon et leurs mots pour rire'. An individual in a quartier he does not know 'se trouve là comme dans un pays lointain'.

If La Bruyère's experience was at all common in the seventeenth and eighteenth centuries, whether in Paris or London, Venice or Naples, it is not difficult to see how the everyday occupations of poor women should have become an object of interest to some upper-class males. Forms of work that were everyday for one group were exotic for another, and working conditions that were experienced as harsh appeared to the outsider to be picturesque. What we see here is a vivid concrete example of what I have described elsewhere as a 'discovery of popular culture' by the elites, a discovery that depended on an earlier 'withdrawal' from participation in the very same culture.[23]

---

[22] Shijian Huang and William Sargent (eds.) *Customs and Conditions of Chinese City Streets* (Shanghai, 1999).
[23] Peter Burke, *Popular Culture in Early Modern Europe* (1978, third edition, Farnham 2009), 23-48, 366-80.

www.ingramcontent.com/pod-product-compliance
Lightning Source LLC
Chambersburg PA
CBHW060956230426
43665CB00015B/2220